BORN IN Madrid in 1883, José Ortega y Gasset was one of the intellectual leaders of the Spanish Republican government. After the establishment of the Republic, Ortega became a member of Parliament. He also held for many years the chair of metaphysics at the University of Madrid and was editor of the influential journal of opinion, *Revista de Occidente*. After the Spanish Civil War, Ortega became an exile from Spain, living for a time in Buenos Aires, later settling in Lisbon. In recent years he visited Spain to lecture in Madrid. *Man and Crisis* was originally published in Spanish under the title of *En Torno A Galileo*. Other books by Ortega include his most widely read work *The Revolt of the Masses, Man and People, Meditations on Quixote, History as a System,* and *What Is Philosophy?*

Señor Ortega died in 1955.

"Ortega y Gasset, after Nietzsche, is perhaps the greatest 'European' writer, and yet it would be difficult to be more Spanish."

—Albert Camus

by JOSÉ ORTEGA Y GASSET

JOSE ORTEGA Y GASSET

MAN AND
CRISIS

TRANSLATED FROM THE SPANISH
BY MILDRED ADAMS

The Norton Library

W · W · NORTON & COMPANY · INC · New York

Contents

Man and Crisis

1

Galileo and His Effect on History

In June of 1633 Galileo Galilei, then seventy years of age, was forced to kneel before the Inquisitorial Tribunal of Rome and renounce the Copernican theory, a concept which was to make possible the modern science of physics.

Three hundred years and more have passed since that deplorable scene, a scene which originated, if the truth be told, more in the small intrigues of private groups than in any dogmatic reservations of the Church. In honor of Galileo I invite you to develop with me certain subjects which are related to the thought of his period.

If we pay homage to Galileo, it is because he interests us as a person. But why does he interest us? Obviously for reasons very different from those for which Galileo interested Galileo. Each of us is interested in himself whether he wishes it or not, whether he thinks himself important or not, and for the simple reason that each of us is both the subject and the protagonist of his own nontransferable life. No one can live my life for me; I myself must go on living it on my own exclusive account, savoring its gaieties, draining its lees, enduring its sorrows, burning with its enthusiasms. Hence no special justification is needed for the fact that each one of us is interested in himself. But some reason is required for our interest in another person, and the more especially when he is not a contemporary. At first sight our interests, our admirations, our curiosities seem to swarm about in a mass which is purely fortuitous. But there is no such thing. Our existence has the quality of an organism and everything in it has its ordained place, its mission, its role to play.

Galileo interests us not merely as such, free and alone, face to face and man to man. As soon as we begin to analyze our interest in his figure, we note that the warmth of that interest increases as we survey him set in a very precise quadrant of history, in a great sector of the past which has a very precise form: the beginning of the modern age, of the system of ideas, values, and forces which fed and dominated the history-laden soil that stretches straight from Galileo to our own feet. Therefore our interest in Galileo is neither so altruistic nor so generous as we might at first imagine. There in the deep background of our contemporary civilization, marked as it is among all the civilizations by the exact natural sciences and the scientific techniques, pulses the man's great figure. He is thus an ingredient in our own lives, and not a casual one, but one whose task it was to play the mysterious role of initiator.

But it is said, and perhaps with no small reason, that all those initiating principles of the modern age now find themselves in a state of crisis. There are many reasons for surmising that European man is lifting his tents from off that modern soil where he has camped these three hundred years and is beginning a new exodus toward another historic ambit, another manner of existence. This would mean that the ground of the modern age which begins beneath the feet of Galileo is coming to an end beneath our own. Our feet have already moved away from it.

But if this be true, the figure of the great Italian takes on an even more dramatic interest for us, concerns us even more intensely. For if it is certain that we are living in a situation of profound historic crisis, that we are surely moving out of one age in order to enter another, it becomes very important for us first, to understand precisely just what is the system of life which we are abandoning; second, to know what it means to live in the midst of an historic crisis; third, to inquire how an historic crisis comes to an end and how we enter into a new age.

The greatest crisis through which the European destiny has ever passed ends with Galileo and Descartes—a crisis which began at the end of the fourteenth century and did not taper off until the early years of the seventeenth century. The figure of Galileo appears at the end of this crisis like a peak between two ages, like a divide that parts the waters. With him modern man enters into the modern age.

It is therefore a matter of supreme interest for us to take this crisis and this entrance into a new period under very close consideration. Every act of entering into any place, every coming out from any corner has about it a bit of the dramatic; at times it has a great deal—hence the rites of the doorway and the lintel. The Romans believed in special gods who presided at that condensation of enigmatic destiny which is the act of going out or of coming in. The god of going out they called *Abeona;* the god of coming in, *Adeona*. If, in place of a pagan god, we speak in Christian terms of a patron saint, nothing would seem more justifiable than to make of Galileo both the *Abeona*, patron saint of our departure from modernity, and the *Adeona*, patron saint of our emergence into a future still palpitant with mystery.

Everyone who has approached the study of that European age which stretches from 1400 to 1600 has noted that of all the periods of our western history this is the most confused; even today it is the least understood. In 1860 Jakob Burckhardt published his book, *Die Kultur der Renaissance in Italien*. For the first time the word *Renaissance,* which had been wandering, vague, and indecisive through the work of Vasari, takes on a precise significance and comes to represent the defining of an historic period. This was a first attempt at the clarification which was to impose order over three centuries of confused recollection. Once again the curious could see that knowledge does not consist in bringing man face to face with an innumerable swarm of raw facts and naked data. Neither the data nor the facts, however accurate, are the veritable stuff of reality itself; in themselves they have no reality, and lacking it, are ill-fitted to convey it to our minds. If the mind, in order to know, had only to reflect a reality which already stood there in the facts, ready as a prudent virgin waiting for her bridegroom, science would be a comfortable task, and man would long ago have discovered all the most urgent truths. But it happens that reality is not a gift which facts make to man. For centuries and centuries the sidereal facts of this world were set clear before the eyes of humans; yet what those facts meant, what they presented to man, what they made evident to him was by no means a reality, but quite the opposite— an enigma, a profound secret, a problem before which man trembled in terror.

Facts, then, come to be like the figures in hieroglyphic writing. Have you ever noted the paradoxical character of such figures? There they are, holding up their clean profiles to us so ostentatiously; but that very appearance of clarity is there for the purpose of presenting us with an enigma, of producing in us not clarity, but confusion. The hieroglyphic figure says to us, "You see me clearly? Good —now what you see of me is not my true being. I am here to warn you that I am not my own essential reality. My reality, my meaning, lies behind me and is hidden by me. In order to arrive at it, you must not fix your attention on me, not take me for reality; on the contrary, you will have to interpret me, and this means that in order to arrive at the true and inward meaning of this hieroglyph, you must search for something very different from the aspect which its figures offer."

Science is the interpretation of facts. By themselves, facts do not give us reality; on the contrary, they hide it, which is to say that they present us with the problem of reality. If there were no facts, there would be no problem, there would be no enigma, there would be nothing hidden which it is necessary to de-hide, to dis-cover. The word which the Greeks used for truth is *aletheia*, which means discovery, to take away the veil that covers and hides a thing. Facts cover up reality; while we are in the midst of their innumerable swarmings we are in chaos and confusion. In order to discover reality we must for a moment lay aside the facts that surge about us, and remain alone with our minds. Then, on our own risk and account, we imagine a reality, or to put it another way, we construct an imaginary reality, a pure invention of our own; then, following in solitude the guidance of our own personal imagining, we find what aspect, what visible shapes, in short, what facts would produce that imaginary reality. It is then that we come out of our imaginative solitude, out from our pure and isolated mental state, and compare those facts which the imagined reality would produce with the actual facts which surround us. If they mate happily one with another, this means that we have deciphered the hieroglyph, that we have discovered the reality which the facts covered and kept secret.

That labor is what science is. As you see, it consists of two different operations: one purely imaginative and creative, which man produces out of his own most free substance; the other a confronting of that which is not man, but of that which surrounds him, the facts, the data. Reality is not a datum, not something given or bestowed, but a construction which man makes out of the given material.

It ought not to be necessary to belabor this. Everyone

who is concerned with scientific work ought to know it. All of modern science has done no other thing than this, and its creators well know that the science of facts, of phenomena, must at a certain moment detach itself from these facts, leave them at one side, and busy itself with the pure process of imagination. Thus, for example, bodies launched into space behave in an innumerable variety of ways—they rise, they fall, they follow in their trajectories the most diverse curves, with very different velocities. In such an immense variety we lose ourselves; and however many observations we make concerning the facts of motion, we fail to discover the true nature of movement. What, on the other hand, did Galileo do? In place of entering the forest of facts as a passive observer and there losing himself, he began by imagining to himself the genesis of the movement of thrown bodies, *cuius motus generationem talem constituo. Mobile quoddam super planum horizontale proiectum mente concipio omni secluso impedimento.*

This is the way Galileo begins the fourth chapter of his last book entitled, *Dialogue of the New Sciences*, or *Discorsi e dimostrazioni matematiche intorno a due nuove scienze attenenti a la mecanica ed i movimenti locali.* The "new sciences" are nothing less than modern physics.

"I conceive as the work of my own mind a moving object launched above a horizontal plane and freed of all impediment." That is to say, an imaginary moving object on a plane which is ideally horizontal and free from any hindrance whatsoever—but those hindrances, those impedimenta from which Galileo imaginatively frees his moving objects are the facts, for every observable body moves in the midst of impedimenta, knocking against other bodies and by other bodies knocked. So he begins by constructing a reality, doing it mentally and ideally. Only when he has his imaginary reality well in hand does he note the facts, or rather, does he observe what relationship obtains between the facts and the imagined reality.

Having that background in mind, I hold the conviction that we are now approaching a splendid flowering of the historic sciences, thanks to the fact that historians will resolve to confront historical facts just as, *mutatis mutandis*, Galileo confronted physical facts. They will become convinced that science—by which I mean the entire body of knowledge about things, whether corporeal or spiritual —is as much a work of imagination as it is of observation, and that the latter is not possible without the former; in short, that science is a process of construction.

The imaginative character of science, imaginative at least in part, makes it a sister of poetry. But between Galileo's imagination and that of a poet lies one fundamental difference—the Galilean imagination is exact and precise. Both the moving object and the horizontal plane which his mind conceived are figures that are rigorously mathematical. But historical material has basically nothing to do with mathematics. Must it therefore renounce all thought of being a construction, which is to say a science, and declare itself to be nothing but poetry? Or is there room for a type of imagination, which, without being mathematical, will lend to history the same strictly constructive service which mechanics renders to physics? Is there room for a quasi mechanics of history?

For the moment we are not going to pursue this question. But I would like to leave in the air, as a kind of hint, certain very general assumptions which, in my judgment, make possible a type of history that is truly scientific.

The historians, to excuse themselves from arguments with the philosophers, customarily repeat a phrase which was written by one of their most able leaders, Leopold de Ranke. His opposition to the discussions of his day in regard to the form of the science of history was expressed (with the air of one hacking irritably at a Gordian knot) in these words: "History proposes to find out *wie es eigentlich gewesen ist,*"—how things actually happened.

At first this phrase seems comprehensible enough; but in view of the controversy which inspired it, its meaning is rather stupid. What happened! What occurred! What was! Which *what?* Is the science of history to occupy itself with the eclipses that have occurred? Obviously not. The phrase is elliptical. One assumes that history deals with what has happened to, what has occurred to, what has befallen, mankind. But this is exactly why, with all due respect to Ranke, whom I believe to be one of the most formidable constructors of history we have, his phrase seems to me a bit stupid. Because what it means is that many things happen to man, an infinite number of things; and these things happen to him in the sense of a roof tile falling on a passerby and breaking his neck. In this type of occurrence man would have no other role than to act as the wall of a handball court, against which hit the fortuitous balls of an extrinsic destiny. History would have no other mission than to record these bouncings, one by one. History would be empiricism, pure and absolute. The human past would be a basic discontinuity of loose facts, without structure, form, or law.

But it is evident that everything which occurs to and happens to a man occurs and happens within his lifetime, and is converted, *ipso facto,* into a fact of human life; this means that the true nature, the reality, of that fact lies not in what it may seem to hold as a raw and isolated happening, but in what it may signify in that man's life. An identical material fact may, if inserted into different human lives, have the most diverse realities. The roof tile which falls is, to a despairing and anonymous passerby, an act of salvation; when it strikes the neck of an empire builder or a young genius it becomes a catastrophe of universal importance.

So a human fact is never a pure matter of happening and befalling—it is a function of an entire human life, individual or collective; it belongs to what one might call an organism of facts in which each one plays its own active and dynamic role. Strictly speaking, the only thing which happens to man is the act of living; all the rest is within his life, sets up reactions in it, has within it a value and a significance. Thus the reality of the fact lies not within the fact itself, but in the indivisible unity of every life.

So that if, following Ranke, we want history to consist in finding out how things actually and truly happened, we have no choice but to turn back from each crude fact to the organic, unitary system of the life to which the fact happened, the life which, so to speak, lived the fact.

So basic is this that the historian cannot read even a single phrase in a document without referring back, if he is to understand it, to the entire life of the document's author. The primary and most elemental task of history is hermeneutic, which is to say interpretive—and, interpretation of the kind that includes every loose and floating fact within the organic structure of a life or of a vital system.

In the light of this observation, which is certainly an obvious one, history ceases to be a simple matter of finding out what happened and is converted into something a bit more complicated—it becomes an investigation into what kind of human lives, and how many of them, have made it up. You will note that I did not say an investigation of what had happened to men—as we have seen, what happens to anyone can be known only when one knows the complete history of the life he has led.

But when history comes up against the great mass of

human lives, it finds itself in the same situation as was Galileo when facing the problem of bodies which move. So many of them move, and in such diverse ways, that we would try in vain to find out from them what movement itself might be. If motion has no structure which is essential and always the same, and of which the individual movements of individual bodies are mere variations and modifications, then a science of physics is impossible. Therefore Galileo had no choice but to begin by setting up a schema, a diagram of motion. That schema would always have to hold true for the movements he was then observing; and thanks to that diagram, we know which are the fundamental movements, how they differ from one another, and why. It is necessary that in the movement of smoke rising from a village chimney and of a stone falling from a tower there be, though seemingly opposite, an identical reality; that is, that the rising and the falling obey the same laws.

Well, then, in the same way the investigation of human lives is not possible if the wide variety in these animals does not hide an identical basic structure; in short, if human life is not, at bottom, the same in the tenth century before Christ as in the tenth century after Christ, among the Chaldeans of Ur as in the Versailles of Louis XV.

The fact is that, whether he knows it or not, every historian approaches the pertinent data carrying in his mind a more or less precise idea of what life is; that is to say, an idea of what are the needs, the possibilities, and the general line of conduct which are characteristic of man. Confronting whatever bit of information a document holds for him, he will pause, and say to himself, "This is not true to life"; that is, this cannot happen to a man, human life excludes certain types of conduct as impossible. But then he goes further. He declares certain of a man's acts to be unlikely, not because they might so be in the absolute, but because they stand in too sharp contradiction to other data about this man's life. And then he says, "This is not true in a man of the tenth century, though it would be very natural in a man of the nineteenth century." Do you not see how the historian, great enemy of philosophy though he be, decides the reality or unreality of a fact by submitting it, as a supreme test, to the idea he holds of a human life as an entirety and an organism?

What I ask of historians is only that they take seriously what they do, what in fact they practice; and in place of constructing history without taking account of what they are doing, they take care to construct it deliberately, starting with a more rigorous idea of the general structure which our life has and which operates identically in all places and at all times.

When one tries to understand a confused, a crisis period —such as the Renaissance—one must start from a clear and precise concept of what life is and what are the functions that make it up. Because this has not been done vigorously and thoroughly, the Renaissance has not been understood, nor have men understood what an historic crisis is. It is therefore essential that we set forth in brief a diagram of human life.

2

The Structure of Life,
The Substance of History

In the previous chapter I suggested that every science which is concerned with reality, whether of the body or of the spirit, must be not merely a mirror of the facts, but a genuine construction. Because the science of physics in the time of Galileo was thus developed, it has endured as a model science and a norm of knowledge for the whole of the modern age.

History must adopt a similar decision and prepare itself to construct. It goes without saying that this comparison between physics as it is and history as it is and as it ought to be is only valid, for the moment, at this single point—the element of construction as such. The other characteristics of physics are not such as to be desirable for history. Take exactitude, for example. The quality of exactitude in physics, that is the exactness of approximation which is proper to it, does not proceed out of its constructive method but comes to it imposed by its object, which is magnitude. The quality of exactness lies not so much in the thinking of the physicist as in the object thought about —the physical phenomenon. So it is a *quid pro quo* to lament the lack of capacity for exactness which will always plague history. The truly lamentable thing would be the exact opposite. If history, which is the science of human lives, were or could be exact, it would mean that men were flints, stones, physiochemical bodies, and nothing else. But then one would have neither history nor physics;

for stones, more fortunate, if you like, than men, do not have to create science in order to be what they are, namely stones. On the other hand man is a most strange entity, who, in order to be what he is, needs first to find out what he is; needs, whether he will or no, to ask himself what are the things around him and what, there in the midst of them, is he. For it is this which really differentiates man from a stone, and not that man has understanding while the stone lacks it. We can imagine a very intelligent stone; but as the inner being of the stone is given it already made, once and for all, and it is required to make no decision on the subject, it has no need, in order to go on being a stone, to pose and pose again the problem of self, asking itself "What must I do now?" or, which is the same thing, "What must I be?" Tossed into the air, without need to ask itself anything, and therefore without having to exercise its understanding, the stone which we are imagining will fall toward the center of the earth. Its intelligence, even if existent, forms no part of its being, does not intervene in it, but would be an extrinsic and superfluous addition.

The essence of man, on the other hand, lies in the fact that he has no choice but to force himself to know, to build a science, good or bad, in order to resolve the problem of his own being and toward this end the problem of what are the things among which he must inexorably have that being. This—that he needs to know, that whether he likes it or not, he needs to work to the best of his intellectual means—is undoubtedly what constitutes the human condition. On the other hand, to define man by saying that he is an intelligent, a rational animal, an animal which knows, *homo sapiens*, is dangerous because, however carefully we use those words, we note that if we ask ourselves "Is any man, even the greatest genius that ever existed, truly and in the fullest meaning of the word, intelligent?

Does he really understand with the required fullness of intelligence, does he really know anything with a complete and unshakable knowing?"—if we ask ourselves this, we note very quickly that the matter is highly dubious and problematical. On the other hand, I repeat, it is beyond question that man needs to know.

Man cannot be defined by listing the talents or the skills on which he counts unless at the same time it is said that those talents, those skills, achieve what their names indicate, and that therefore they are adequate to the frightening task into which, whether he likes it or not, man finds himself thrust. Or to put it another way, man does not busy himself in learning, in comprehending, simply *because* he has talents and intelligence which enable him to know and to understand, but on the contrary; for the very reason that he has no choice but to try to comprehend, to know, he mobilizes all the abilities of which he stands possessed, even though for that necessity these may serve him very badly. If man's intelligence were truly what the word indicates—the capacity to understand—he would at once have understood everything, and would have no problem, no laborious task ahead of him. So then, it is not said that man's intelligence is actually intelligence; on the other hand, there is no doubt about the task in which man is irremediably engaged, and therefore it is surely that task which defines his destiny.

That task, as we have said, is called "living"; the essence of living is that man is always existing within an environment, that he finds himself—suddenly and without knowing how he got there—projected into and submerged in a world, a set of fixed surroundings, into this present, which is now about us.

In order to sustain himself in that environment he is always having to do something. But this something is not imposed on him by the surrounding environment as is a phonograph's repertoire by the disks it plays, or as the line which a star traces is imposed by its orbit.

Man, every man, must at every moment be deciding for the next moment what he is going to do, what he is going to be. This decision only he can make; it is not transferable; no one can substitute for me in the task of deciding for myself, in deciding on my life. When I put myself into another's hands, it is I who have decided and who go on deciding that he will direct me; thus I do not transfer the decision itself, but merely its mechanism. In place of deriving the norm of my conduct out of that mechanism which is my own intelligence, I take advantage of the mechanism of another's intelligence.

But if, on closing this book, you go in one direction rather than another, it is because you think you ought to go to a certain place at a certain hour, and this in turn you decided for another reason concerned with the future, and so on successively. Man cannot take a single step without anticipating more or less clearly his entire future, what he is going to be; that, is, what he has decided to be throughout his life. But this means that man, who is always obliged to do something in the circumstances that surround him, has in deciding what he is going to do no other course than to pose to himself the problem of his own individual being. When we meet a neighbor it does not take great perspicacity to note how he is guided by that self which he himself has chosen, but which he never sees clearly, which always remains a problem to him. For when each one of us asks himself what he is going to be, and therefore what his life is going to be, he has no choice but to face the problem of man's being, of what it is that man in general can be and what is it that he must be. But this, in turn, obliges us to fashion for ourselves an idea, to find out somehow what this environment is, what these surroundings are, this world in which we live. The things about us do not of themselves tell us what they are. We must discover that for ourselves. But this—to discover the self of things and of one's own being, the being of everything—this is none other than man's intellectual business, a task which is therefore not an extrinsic and superfluous addition to man's life, but a constituent part of that life. This is not a matter of man's living and then, if it falls out that way, if he feels some special curiosity, of busying himself in formulating ideas about the things around him. No; to live is to find oneself forced to interpret life. Always, irresistibly, moment by moment we find ourselves with definite and fundamental convictions about what things are and what we ourselves are in the midst of them; this articulation of final convictions is what molds our chaotic surroundings into the unity of a world or a universe.

What we have been saying presents us with our lives made up of two dimenisons, the one inseparable from the other; this I would like to leave with you, emphatic and completely clear. In its primary dimension, to live is to be myself, the "I" which is each one of us, in the environment which surrounds us, and with no choice but to cope with it. But this imposes on life a second dimension, consisting of the need to find out what the environment is. In its first dimension, what we have in living is pure problem. In its second dimension we have an intent or an effort to resolve the problem. We think about our environment, and this thinking creates for us an idea, a map, an architectural design of the pure problem, of the chaos which in the first instance our surroundings appear to be. This architectural design which thought lays over our surroundings, interpreting them, we call *world*, or *universe*. This is not given to us, nor is it simply there; it is created by our convictions.

There is no way of bringing a bit of clarity into the

problem of what human life is unless we take into account the fact that the world, the universe, is the intellectual solution with which man reacts to the given problems, inexorable and inescapable, which are posed for him by his surroundings. It follows that: first, what the solutions may be depends on what the problems are; second, a solution is genuine only insofar as the problem is genuine, that is to say, insofar as we find ourselves actually worried over it. When, for one reason or another, we cease to feel the problem deeply, the solution, however apt, loses its importance for us, ceases to play the role of a solution, and becomes a dead idea.

I wanted to emphasize all this because it shows so vividly the duality which is inherent in human living; by virtue of this duality man is always in the midst of the problem which his surroundings set for him, but, forced to react to this problem, he is also always in the midst of a relative solution. The most skeptical of us live amid certain fundamental convictions, live in a world, in an interpretation. The skeptic's world is called "the doubtful"; he lives in it, he exists within that doubt, in a sea of doubts, in a sea of confusions, as the common phrase describes it. That world of the doubtful, however frighteningly poor it may be, is as much of a world as is the world of the dogmatic. When one speaks, then, of a "man without convictions" let him note with care that this is merely a manner of speaking. There is no life without ultimate certainties; the very skeptic himself is convinced that everything is doubtful.

When I pointed out that our life, the life of every one of us, is perforce an interpretation of itself, is a forming of ideas about itself and about everything else, the reader will have said to himself that he had never realized he made such an effort. And he is right, if he understood my words to mean that each man by his own individual effort creates for himself an interpretation of the universe. Unfortunately, or fortunately, that is not what happens. As soon as we find ourselves living, we find ourselves not only among things but also among men, not only on earth, but also in society. And those men, that society into which we have fallen by the process of being alive, already has its own interpretation of life, its repertory of ideas, of ruling convictions about the universe. So that what we can call "the thought of our time" enters to form part of our surroundings; it envelops us, it penetrates into us, it carries us. One of the factors that makes up our destiny is the mass of circumambient convictions in which we find ourselves. Without realizing it, we find ourselves installed in that network of ready-made solutions for the problems of our lives. When one of these problems weighs on us, we revert to that treasure, asking our neighbors, or the books that they read, "What is the world? What is man? What is death? What lies beyond?" Or perhaps "What is space?" "What is light?" "What is the animal organism?" Nor is it necessary to ask such questions; from the very moment of birth—in family life, in school, in reading, and in social intercourse—we are constantly trying to receive and absorb those collective convictions into our veins before, almost always before, we have become aware of the problems for which they are, or pretend to be, solutions. So that when we come to feel actual distress in the face of a vital question, and we really want to find its solution, to orient ourselves with respect to it, not only must we struggle with the problem, but we find ourselves caught within the solutions previously received and must also struggle with them. The very language in which we will have to think our own thoughts is itself an alien way of thinking, a collective philosophy, an elementary interpretation of the life which so closely imprisons us.

We have seen how the concept of the world or the

universe is the map which man forms for himself, willy-nilly, in order to walk among things and to realize his life, in order to orient himself amid the chaos of surrounding circumstances. But that concept is given to him by his human environment, it is the idea which is dominant in his time. With it he must live, either accepting it or arguing against it on this point or that.

In addition to thinking about things or knowing about them, man makes implements, fashions tools, lives, so far as matter is concerned, with a technique. His circumstances differ according to the degree of technical excellence which he finds about him at birth. Modern man is not weighed down by material problems as was paleolithic man. He devotes himself to other kinds. The fundamental structure of his life is the same, but the appearance of his problems is different. Life is always preoccupation, but in each period some things worry man more than others. Smallpox, for example, which was a serious concern in 1850, is not one of today's worries. Today, on the other hand, parliamentary rule, which was no worry in those earlier days, now perturbs us deeply.

Having scanned the surface of the matter, we now find ourselves with these clear truths: first, that every man's life starts with certain basic convictions about what the world is and what man's place in it is—it starts from these and moves within them; second, every life finds itself in surroundings which include more or less technical skill or control over the material environment.

Here are two permanent functions, two essential factors in all human life which are mutually influential—ideology and technique.

A complete study would lead us to discover the remaining dimensions of life. But for the time being these two are enough, for they allow us to glimpse the fact that human life always has a structure—that is to say, it consists in man's having to cope with a predetermined world of which we can sketch the profile. The world presents certain problems which, relatively speaking, are solved, and raises others, thus giving a definite aspect to man's struggle for his own fate.

History busies itself with finding out what human lives were like; but the expression is usually misunderstood, as though this were a matter of inquiring into the character of the human subjects. Life is not solely man, that is to say, the subject which lives. It is also the drama which arises when that subject finds himself obliged to fling his arms about, to swim shipwrecked in that sea which is the world. History, then, is not primarily the psychology of man, but the refashioning of the structure of that drama which flares between man and the world. In a specific world, confronted by it, men of the most diverse psychologies find themselves possessed of a common and inevitable repertory of problems which gives to their existences an identical basic structure. The psychological differences, subjective in nature, are subordinate, and do no more than bring minor deviations to the plot of their common drama.

To make my thinking clear, let me give you an example. Imagine two individuals of opposite temperaments, one very gay, the other very sad, but both living in a world where God exists and in which material techniques are elementary. (In general, the periods having a deep concern with God are periods of a backward technique, and vice versa). At first we tend to attribute great importance in the configuration of both lives to this difference in character. But if we then compare one of these men, the gay one, for example, with another as gay as he but living in a different world, a world in which there is no God, but which has a highly developed technical civilization, we note that in spite of the fact that they both enjoy the same temperament, their lives differ far more than do those of that other pair who differ in character but are submerged in the same world.

History must abandon the devotion to psychology, the subjectivism in which its finest modern productions are losing themselves, and must recognize that its mission is to reconstruct the objective conditions in which individuals, the human subjects, have been submerged. From now on its basic question must be, not how human beings have differed, but how the objective structure of life has varied.

Each one of us today finds himself submerged in a system of problems, perils, things that are easy and things that are hard, possibilities and impossibilities which are not one's self but the thing within which one exists, with which one must contend; and in the management of these things, or the struggle with them, one's very life consists. Had we been born a hundred years ago, though possessing the same characters and identical talents, the drama of our lives would have been very different.

The fundamental question of history comes down to this, then: What changes have there been in the vital life structure? How, when, and why does life change?

3

The Idea of the Generation

___

THE same thing may be thought about in two ways—from the inside or the outside, *in vacuo* or in the round. If we say that history proposes to find out how human lives have been lived, one can be sure that he who listens to us, understanding these words and repeating them to himself, will think of them *in vacuo;* that is, he will not bring before himself the reality which is human life, will not actually think of the content of that idea, but will use these words as an empty container, a hollow flagon which carries on its outside a label reading "human life." It is as if he said "All right, I recognize that in thinking about these words now—on reading them, hearing them, pronouncing them—I do not really have before me the thing they signify; but I am confident that whenever I want to stop to realize what they mean, to bring before myself the reality they denote, I could do it. So I use them in a fiduciary sense, on credit, as I use a check, sure that whenever I want to I can exchange it at the bank window for the cash money which it represents. I confess that, strictly speaking, I am not thinking my idea through, but am merely considering its shell, its capsule, its void."

This thinking in the void and on credit, thinking something without actually thinking it through, is our usual way of thinking. The advantage of the words which offer material support to thought has the disadvantage that they tend to supplant that thought; and if some fine day we should set ourselves to plumb the repertory of our most customary and habitual thoughts, we would find ourselves painfully surprised to discover that we do not have actual thoughts but merely the words for them, or certain vague images attached to them; so that we have only the checks, and not the actual cash money they pretend to be worth; in short, that intellectually we are like banks in pseudo bankruptcy. Pseudo, because each one lives with his thoughts; and if these are false and empty, he is falsifying his life and swindling himself.

In the two previous chapters I have tried to make it easy for you to fill the words "human life" with reality— words which to us are perhaps the most important in the entire dictionary because that reality is not just any reality, but our own, and in being ours it is the one in which all the others are included as our own, the reality of all the realities. Everything which in any sense pretends to be a reality must somehow appear within my life.

But human life is not a reality directed toward the outside—the life of every one of you is not merely what I see by looking at you from within myself. On the contrary, what I see of you is not *your* life, but a portion of my own. To have you there as readers, to be talking to you on paper, is something that is happening to me. I find you facing me in various guises—young people who are studying, older men and women—and on speaking to you I find myself obliged, among other things, to search for a way of expression which will be comprehensible to all of you; that is to say, I must consider you, must deal with you, so that you are, for the moment, an element in my destiny, in my surroundings. But it is clear that the life of every one of you is to you not what each of you is to me, turning toward me and therefore toward something outside yourselves, but it is what each of you lives for yourself, out of yourself, and directed toward yourself. And in that life of yours I am no more than one ingredient in your destiny, an ingredient of the environment in which you live. For each of you, life at this moment consists in having to sit there reading what I say; and this even though some of you may not have picked up this book especially to read me, but for any number of other reasons which I will not enumerate, although I could. Even in that case your life now consists in having to pay attention to what I write, whether you like it or not, for in order not to read me while you have my pages in your hand you must undertake the painful effort of unreading me, of managing to detach yourself from my pages by concentrating your attention on something else—as we so often do in order to defend ourselves against those two new enemies of man, the phonograph and the radio.

The reality of a life, then, consists not in what it is for him who sees it from the outside, but in what it is for him who is within it, for him who goes on living it, while and insofar as he lives it. Hence, in order to know another life which is not ours, we must try to see it not from within ourselves but from the point of view of the person who lives it.

This is why I said very formally, and not as a matter of simple metaphor, that life is drama; the character of its reality is not like the reality of this table, which consists merely in being here, but is made up of the fact that each one must go on doing for himself, moment after moment, in a perpetual tension of affliction and hardship, without ever having complete security within himself. Is not this the very definition of drama? Drama is not a thing which is there—it is not in any real sense a thing, a static being— but drama happens, it occurs—that is, it is the happening of something to someone, it is that which is happening to someone, it is that which is happening to the protagonist while it is going on.

But even while saying that life is drama we usually misunderstand the phrase, interpreting it as though it meant that in the process of living we are used to having drama happen to us from time to time; or better, that living is having many things happen to one—for instance, having a toothache or winning a prize in a lottery, lacking enough to eat, falling in love with a woman, or feeling an unconquerable desire to be a minister of state, to be, *velis nobis,* a student in the university, and so on. But this would mean that drama, big or little, tragic or comic, happens *in* life; not that life is essentially and solely drama. And this is precisely what I am saying. Because all the other things that occur and that happen to us do so because one single thing is happening to us—the act of living. If we were not living, nothing would be happening to us; on the other hand, because we are living, and only *because* we are living, do all the various things happen to us.

Now then, that unique and essential "happening to us," which is the cause of all the rest—the act of living—has one most peculiar condition, and that is that we always have in our own hands the power to make it not happen. Men can always stop living. It is painful to bring in the possibility, always open to man, of fleeing from life; it is painful, but it is necessary. For this and this alone uncovers a most primary and vital characteristic of our life, which is this: we did not give it to ourselves, but we met it for ourselves, or we found ourselves in it when we first became aware of ourselves—yet on finding ourselves in life, we might very well abandon it. If we do not abandon it, this is because we want to live. But then, note what follows: if, as we have seen, everything happens to us because the fact of living is happening to us, as we accept this essential happening by wishing to live, it is evident that everything else that happens to us, however adverse or desperate it may be, happens to us because we desire it—that is, because we want to go on being. Man is the hunger to be—the absolute passionate desire to be, to subsist—and the desire to be as he is, to realize his most highly individual "I."

But this has two faces: an entity made up of the desire to be, consisting in the strenuous struggle to be, is evidently already in existence; if not, it could not struggle. This on the one hand. But on the other, what is that entity? We have already described it as the eager effort to be. All right; but only he can feel the effort to be who is not quite sure of being, who feels it constantly problematical as to whether he may or may not, in the next moment or so, continue to be, and whether he will be this kind of a being or that. Hence our life is the hunger to be for the very reason that it is at the same time, and at bottom, fundamentally insecure. Hence we are always doing something to assure ourselves of life; and first of all we formulate an interpretation of the environment in which we must have our being and of ourselves as we expect to go on being in it—we define the horizon within which we must live.

That interpretation takes form within what we call "our convictions"—what we believe ourselves to be certain of, what we know we can depend on. And that complex of certainties which, in thinking about the environment, we build for ourselves—like a raft in the tempestuous and enigmatic sea of our surroundings—this complex is the world, the vital horizon. Whence it happens that in order to live man needs, whether he likes it or not, to think, to form convictions for himself—or, what is the same thing, to live is to react against the basic insecurity of life by constructing the security of a world, by believing that the world is like this or like that so that we may direct our lives with due regard for it, so that in view of it we may live.

We discarded the definition of man as *homo sapiens*

because it seemed to us compromising and excessively optimistic. So man knows? At the time I am writing, and taking a look at modern humanity, that question is much too disquieting; for if anything is at this moment clear, it is that man, and the very man who is most civilized, on this continent or any other, does not know what to do.

Those earlier considerations would lead us to take shelter in the other old definition which describes man as *homo faber*, the being that fabricates, or as Franklin said, the animal that makes tools—*animal instrumentificum*. But we would have to give that idea a very basic meaning which its authors never suspected. It means that man is capable of fabricating instruments, tools, useful things which help him to live. He is capable—but reality is not defined by what one is capable of doing but very well may not do. Nowadays we are not fabricating tools in the sense which that definition used to have; yet nevertheless we are men. But, I repeat, it is possible to give this definition a much broader meaning; man is always, at every moment, living according to what the world is to him; you have acquired this book and are now reading it, because within your world this seems to make sense to you. Therefore, in this act of doing which is the process of having got the book, of holding it, and turning your attention to my work, you are carrying out your concept of the world, that is, you are for the moment making a world, giving force to a certain world. And I would say the same thing if in place of reading this book you were doing something else in another place. You would always do it by virtue of the world or the universe in which you believe, of which you think. Except that in a concrete and specific case like ours, the matter is even clearer and more literal; because many of you are reading to see if you will find out anything new about what the world is, to see if, together, we can make the world a bit new although we merely touch on one of its dimensions, quadrants, or sectors.

Whatever his degree of energy, ability, or originality, man is constantly fabricating a world; we have already seen that the world or indeed the universe is nothing more than the schema or the interpretation with which he arms himself to assure himself of life. Let us then say that the world is the instrument *par excellence* which man produces, and that the act of producing it is one and the same thing as his life, his being. Man is born a fabricator of universes.

Here you have the reason why there is history and why there is such continuous variation in human life. If we cut into the human past at any particular date we always find man installed in a particular world, as in a house which he has made to shelter himself from the elements. In the face of certain problems which the environment poses for him that world gives him a sense of security; but it also leaves many unsolved problems, many perils which he can neither resolve nor avoid. His life, the drama of his life, will have a different profile according to the look of the problems, according to the balance between the elements of security and uncertainty which that world represents.

We are now in a position of relative security insofar as the danger that a star may collide with the earth and destroy it. Why this security? Because we believe in a world which is sufficiently rational to make possible the science of astronomy; and astronomy assures us that so far as our lives are concerned the probabilities of such a collision are practically nil. More than that, the astronomers, who have always been wonderful people, have entertained themselves by counting the number of years which are still to go before a star whirls into the sun and destroys it; this would be exactly a billion two hundred and three years. We can still go on talking a while longer.

But now imagine that natural phenomena should suddenly begin to contravene the laws of physics—that is, that we should lose confidence in science, which is, incidentally, the faith by which modern European man lives. We would find ourselves facing an irrational world, that is to say, a world not to be plumbed by our scientific reasoning, which is the only thing that makes it possible for us to assure ourselves of a certain dominance over material circumstances. *Ipso facto*, our life, our human drama would undergo a profound change of face —our life would be a very different life because we would be living in another world. The house in which we had installed ourselves would fall in. In material matters we would no longer know what we could trust; and the human being would again be cursed by the terrible blight which for thousands of years caught him by the throat and held him prisoner—that cosmic horror, that panic terror, the fear of Pan.

Well then; this thing is not so completely remote from reality as one might suppose. These days civilized man is feeling a terror of which, only thirty years ago, he was completely ignorant. Thirty years ago he believed himself to be living in a world where economic progress was without finite limits and free from serious lapses. But in these last years the world has changed; young men whose lives began amid ample circumstances now live in a world of economic crisis which sets every element of security in this sector of life to wobbling—and which may carry in its train many unsuspected and well-nigh incredible changes in human life.

This makes it possible for us to formulate two fundamental principles for the construction of history: (1) Man is continually making a world, hammering out a horizon; (2) Every change in the world, every shift of horizon, brings with it a change in the structure of the vital drama. The psycho-physiological entity which has life, the body and the soul of man, cannot change; nevertheless his life changes because the world has changed. And man is not his body and soul but his life, the embodiment of his life problem.

The theme of history is thus formally determined and defined as the study of the forms or structures which human life has taken since we had any information about it.

But it will be said that life is always and continually changing its structure. Because if we said that man is constantly making the world, that means that the world is constantly being modified and therefore that the structure of life will be endlessly changing. In the last analysis this is certainly true. In preparation for this chapter I had to think out with more precision certain points about what I believe to be the historic world, which is none other than a portion of my world. Therefore this has been modified in certain details. Similarly I hope that this chapter may exert a change, however slight, on some aspect of the world in which you were living when you picked up this book a while ago. Yet the general architecture of the universe in which you and I were living yesterday remains intact. The material of which the walls of our houses are made changes a little every day. Yet provided that we have not moved out, we have the right to say that we are inhabiting the same house as we did years ago. There is no reason for exaggerating the strict accuracy of the statement, for that would lead us into a false position. When the modifications suffered by the world in which I believe do not affect its principal elements of construction, and its general profile remains intact, man has no impression that the world has changed, but only that something in the world has changed.

But another highly obvious consideration puts us on the track of what the kind of modifications are which must be valued as constituting an effective change in the horizon or the world. History is not occupied solely with individual life as such; even when an historian proposes to write a biography he finds the life of his subject entangled with the lives of other men, and their lives, in turn, with the lives of others—which is to say that each life is submerged in a specific environment of a collective life. And this collective, this anonymous life in which each of us finds himself also has its world, its repertory of convictions, of which, whether he likes it or not, the individual must take account. More than that, this world of collective beliefs—which are usually called "the ideas of the period," "the spirit of the times"—has a peculiar character not possessed by the world of individual beliefs; namely, it is valid for itself regardless of and sometimes despite our acceptance of it. A conviction of mine, no matter how firm it may be, has validity only for me. But the concepts of the time, the ambient convictions, are held by an anonymous subject who is no one in particular; this is society. And those concepts have force and validity even though I may not accept them—that force makes itself felt on me, even though negatively. There they are, ineluctable, as that wall is there; and whether I like it or not, I must take account of them in my life, just as I must take account of the wall which will not let me pass through it, but obliges me to seek the door or else to spend a portion of my life in demolishing it. But it is clear that the greatest influence which the spirit of the times, the world in force, exerts on each individual life is exercised not by the simple fact of being there (or what is the same, for the reason that I am in it, and in it I must move and have my being) but because the greater portion of my world, of my beliefs, arises out of that collective repertory, and coincides with its contents. The spirit of the times, the greater portion of the ideas of the period, are in me, they are mine. From the moment of birth man goes on absorbing the convictions of his time, that is to say, he continues to find himself in the world "in force."

This, simple as it is, sheds a decisive light on the changes which are properly called historic, on the kind of modifications which we must consider as effective changes in the world and therefore in the structure of the life drama.

Until he is twenty-five years old, man normally does little but learn, receive information about the things that make up his social environment—his teachers, the books, the conversations that surround him. In those years he becomes aware of what the world is, he comes up against the aspects of a world which he finds already made. But that world is merely the system of convictions in force at that date. The system of convictions has gone on being formed over the course of a very long past, and some of its most elemental components come down from primitive humanity. But the facets of that world which are most vivid, the affairs in it which are most compelling, have received a new interpretation from the men who represent the maturity of that period, and who act as the administrators of that period in all its categories—in the universities, the newspapers, the government, in literary and artistic life. As man is always making a world, those mature men have produced this or that modification in the horizon which they found. The young man finds himself caught in this world at twenty-five, and throws himself into living in it on his own account, that is to say, he too takes his place in world-making. But as he meditates on the world in force (the world of the men who in his time are mature) his thesis, his problems, his doubts, are very different from those which these mature men felt when in their own youth they in turn meditated on the world of those who were then mature (men who are now very old), and so on backwards.

If we are considering only one or two young men who react to the world of the mature, the modifications to which their meditations will lead them will be very few, possibly important at some point, but in the last analysis only partial. One could not say that their activity changes the world.

But this is not a matter of just a few young men; it touches all those who are young at a certain date, who are rather more in number than the ones who are mature. Each youth will be particularly active at one point of the horizon; but between them they will bring pressure to bear on the entire horizon,—some of them on art, others on religion or one of the sciences, on industry, on politics. The modifications which they produce at each point have to be minimal; yet we must recognize that they have changed the whole face of the world so that years later, when another crowd of youngsters start their life, they will find themselves with a world looking entirely different from what it did when their elders met it.

The most elemental fact of human life is that some men die and others are born—that lives succeed each other. All human life, in its very essence, is boxed in between other lives which came before or which are to come after —it proceeds out of one life and goes into one which is to follow. It is on this most fundamental fact that I base the inevitable necessity of change in the structure of the world. An automatic mechanism drags with it the irremediable certainty that within a given unit of time the characters of the life drama change, much as characters change in those theatres devoted to short skits and presenting a different comedy or tragedy every hour. One need not assume that the actors are different—the same actors *must* play different parts. This is not to say that the youth of today is different either in body or in soul from the youth of yesterday, but it is inevitable that his life should have a different framework.

What we are doing is finding the reason for historic changes and the period in which they take place in the fact tied most closely to human life, namely, that life always has a length of years, an age. Life is time, as Dilthey made us see and as Heidegger repeats to us today; and not cosmic time which is imaginary and therefore infinite, but limited time, time which comes to an end, time which is the true and irreparable time. Because of this man has an age. Age is the fact of man's being always in a certain sector of his scanty time-span, whether this be the beginning of his life's time, the climb toward its noon tide, its center, or the approach toward its end—in more customary terms, whether he is a child, a youth, a grown man, or an old man.

But this means that every historic present, every "today," involves three distinct times, three different "todays." Or, to put it another way: the present is rich in three great vital dimensions which dwell together in it, whether they will or no, linked with one another, and perforce, because they are different, in essential hostility one to the other. For some, "today" is the state of being twenty, for others, forty, and for still another group, sixty; and this, the fact that three such very different ways of life have the same "today," creates the dynamic drama, the conflict, and the collision which form the background of historic material and of all modern living together. And in the light of this observation, one sees the ambiguity which is hidden in the apparent clarity of the date as such. 1933 seems a single time; but in 1933 there lived a boy, a mature man, and an old man, and that set of digits is at once tripled in three different meanings, and at the same time embraces all three; it is the unity of three different ages in one historic time.

We are all contemporaries, we live at the same time, in the same atmosphere—in the same world—but we contribute to their forming in very different ways. This way is identical only for coevals. Contemporaries are not coevals. In history it is important to distinguish between that which is contemporary and that which is coeval. Dwelling in the same external and chronological time, they live together in three very different periods of life. This is what I usually call the essential anachronism of history. Thanks to that internal disequilibrium, it moves, changes, wheels, and flows. If all of us who are contemporaries were also coevals, history would be stopped in a state of paralysis, petrified, having only one face, with no possibility of radical innovation.

Well, then; the group of those who are coevals in the circle of modern living together is what is called a generation. The concept of generation does not primarily imply more than these two things: to be of the same age and to have some vital contact. There still remain on this planet human groups which are isolated from all the others. It is obvious that the individuals in those groups who are of the same age as we are do not belong to our generation because they take no part in our world. But this in turn means (1) that if every generation has a dimension in historic time, that is to say in the melody of the human generations, it comes directly after another of its kind, as the note of a song sounds in relation to the way the previous note sounded; (2) that it also has a dimension in space.

At each and every date the circle of human living is broad or narrow. At the dawn of the Middle Ages the territories which had lived together in historic contact during the good days of the Roman Empire appear, for very curious reasons, disassociated, each one submerged and absorbed within itself. This was a period of dispersed and discontinuous multiplicity. Almost every clod lived solely to itself. This produced a marvelous diversity of human ways which gave birth to the nationalities. During the Empire, on the contrary, there was a general living together which extended from the frontier of India to Lisbon, to England, and to the other side of the Rhine. This was a period of uniformity; and although difficulties of communication gave that living together a highly relative character, one could say that in terms of ideas all the coevals from London to the river Pontus formed a single generation. And to belong to a generation which is broadly uniform is to have a very different vital destiny, a very different life structure, from belonging to one which is narrow, heterogeneous, and dispersed. And there are generations whose destiny it is to break through a people's isolation and to lead them to live spiritually with others, thus integrating them into a much broader unity, taking them out of their retrograde history, freeing them from being individual and housebound, so to speak, and introducing them into the gigantic ambit of universal history.

Community of date and of space are, I repeat, the primary attributes of a generation. Together they signify the sharing of an essential destiny. The keyboard of environment on which coevals must play the *sonata apassionata* of their lives is in its fundamental structure one and the same. This identity of destiny produces in coevals certain secondary coincidences which are summed up in the unity of their vital style.

At one time I pictured a generation as "a caravan within which man moves a prisoner, but at the same time, a voluntary one at heart, and content. He moves within it faithful to the poets of his age, to the political ideas of his time, to the type of woman triumphant in his youth, and even to the fashion of walking which he employed at twenty-five. From time to time he sees another caravan pass with a strange and curious profile; this is the other generation. Perhaps celebrations on a feast day may bring the two together, may blend them; but as the hour of normal living approaches the somewhat chaotic fusion divides into two organic groups. Each individual mysteriously recognizes all of the rest of his collectivity, as the ants in each ant hill recognize each other by a peculiar pattern of odor.

"The discovery that we are fatally inscribed within a certain group having its own age and style of life is one of the melancholy experiences which, sooner or later, befalls every sensitive man. A generation is an integrated manner of existence, or, if you prefer, a fashion in living, which fixes itself indelibly on the individual. Among certain savage peoples the members of each coeval group are recognized by their tattooing. The fashion in epidermal design which was in vogue when they were adolescents has remained encrusted in their beings."

In the "today," in every "today," various generations coexist and the relations which are established between them, according to the different condition of their ages, represent the dynamic system of attractions and repulsions, of agreement and controversy, which at any given moment makes up the reality of historic life. The concept of the generations, converted into a method of historic investigation, consists in nothing more than projecting that structure across the past. Everything else is a refusal to discover the authentic reality of human life at a given time, a renouncing of the mission of history. The method of the generations allows us to see that life from within itself, as it actually is. History is the virtual converting of that which has passed into that which is present. Therefore—and not only as a matter of metaphor—history is a reliving, a reviving, of the past. And as living is nothing else but actuality and the present, we must travel back from the actuality and the present which are ours to those which went before, looking at them not from without, not as conditions of living which have been, but as those which continue to be alive.

But now we need to define this matter a little more closely.

The generation, we were saying, is the aggregate of men who are the same age.

Unlikely as it may seem, men have tried to reject the method of the generations *a limine* by opposing to it the ingenious observation that men are born every day, and that therefore only those who are born on the same day are, strictly speaking, of the same age; therefore that the generation is an illusion, an arbitrary concept which does not represent a reality, and that, if we employ it, this technique conceals and deforms reality. History has need of a peculiar exactitude, historical exactitude, which is not in any sense mathematical; when one tries to replace the one with the other, one falls into errors like this objection, which might well have gone to a further extreme by restricting the number of coevals to those born in the same hour or at the same minute.

But it would be useful to take into account the fact that the concept of age is not the stuff of mathematics, but of life. Age is not, in point of origin, a date. Long before men knew how to count, society appeared—and among primitive peoples still appears—organized into classes identified by age. So much is this most elemental fact of life a reality that it spontaneously gives form to the social body, dividing it into three or four groups according to the length of personal existence. Within the human trajectory of life, age is a certain way of living—inside the totality of our lives, there is, so to speak, a life with its beginning and its end: one begins to be young and one ceases to be young, as one begins to live and finishes living. And that manner of life which age is—measured externally according to the chronology of cosmic time, which is not vital time but time as measured by watches—is spread over a series of years. One is young not only for a single year, nor is one young only at twenty and not at twenty-two. One continues to be young throughout a definite series of years just as one lives in the midst of maturity for a certain period of cosmic time.

Age, then, is not a date, but a "zone of dates"; and it is not only those born in the same year who are the same age in life and in history, but those who are born within a zone of dates.

If each of you will go back over those whom you regard as coevals, as members of your own generation, you will find that you do not know the age-year of those acquaintances, but you will be able to fix a set of upper and lower limits and measuring by them say "so and so is not of my time, he is still a boy"—or "he is already an adult."

So it is not by putting our trust in strict mathematical chronology that we can fix ages.

In earlier days, before mathematics had laid waste the spirit of life, there in the ancient world and the Middle Ages and even at the dawn of the modern world, the sages and the ingenious both meditated on this great question. There was a theory of man's ages, and Aristotle, for example, did not scorn to dedicate certain splendid pages to it.

There are answers for all tastes. Human life has been

divided into three or four ages, but also into five, into seven, and even into ten. Shakespeare, in *As You Like It*, championed the division into seven.

> All the world's a stage,
> And all the men and women merely players.
> They have their exits and their entrances
> And one man in his time plays many parts,
> His acts being seven ages.

But it is undeniable that only the divisions into three and four have had any permanence in man's interpretations. Both are enshrined in Greece and in the Orient, as in the primitive Germanic background. Aristotle is a partisan of the simplest type—youth, maturity (or *akme'*), and old age. On the other hand, one of Aesop's fables, which combines Oriental and Germanic elements, tells us of four ages: "God wanted man and the animals to have the same length of life—thirty years. But the animals observed that this seemed too long a time to them, while it seemed very little to man. Then they came to an accord, and the donkey, the dog, and the monkey agreed to hand over part of their years to be added to those of man. In this way the human being achieves a life of seventy years. The first thirty are good years, and in them man enjoys good health, he amuses himself, he works joyfully, happy in his destiny. But then come the eighteen years of the donkey, when he has to bear load after load, he must carry the grain which someone else eats, and endure kicks and beatings in return for his good service. Then come the twelve years of the dog's life; he crawls into a corner, growls, and shows his teeth, though he has very few teeth left for biting. And when this has passed, then come the ten years of the monkey, which are the last; man makes whistling noises and foolish gestures, busies himself with absurd manias, goes bald, and is useful only as a butt for the laughter of little children."

This fable, with its unhappy caricatured reality bearing the marks of the Middle Ages, shows very sharply how the concept of man's various ages is formed primarily on the various periods in the life drama, which are not digits, not dates, but modes of living. Plutarch, in his life of Lycurgus, quotes three lines, which are supposed to be recited each by a chorus:

The Old Man: We were young once, and brave and strong.
The Young Man: And so we're now—come on and try.
The Children: But we'll be strongest, by and by.

I bring forth these allusions and I give you these quotations so that you may see the deep echo which this theme of the ages has stirred in man's heart since the most remote time.

But up to now the concept of age has preoccupied man only from the point of view of the individual life. Hence, among other things, the vacillation about the cycle and character of the ages—boys, youths, old men, as in the citation from Plutarch; youth, maturity, age, decrepitude, as in Aesop's fable; youth, adult, old man, as in Aristotle.

We will start the next chapter with an attempt to fix the ages and the time of each one from the point of view of history. This is a matter for historic reality, not for us, to decide.

4

The Method of the Generations in History

AT any given moment man lives in a world of convictions, the greater part of which are the convictions common to all men who dwell together in their era. This spirit of the times we have called the world "in force," the ruling world, in order to show that it has not only the reality which our conviction lends to it, but also that it imposes itself upon us, whether we like it or not, as the most important ingredient in our surroundings. Just as man finds himself encased within the body which has fallen to him by chance and must live in it and with it, so he finds himself with the ideas of his time, and in them and with them—even though it be in the peculiar fashion of contending against them—must he live. The *mundo vigente*, that world in force, that spirit of the times—with which and in the operation of which we live, in view of which we decide our simplest actions—is the variable element of human life. When it changes, so does the argument of the human drama. Important modifications in the structure of human life depend much more on this change in the world than on a shift of characters, races, etc. And as the theme of history is not human life, which is an affair of philosophy, but the changes, the variations in human life, we will hold that the primordial factor of history is the world which is "in force" in each period.

But that world changes with every generation for the

very reason that the previous generation has done something in the world, has left it somewhat different from the way it found it. The Madrid which those who are twenty years old find today is different, even visually, from what it was when my own blossoming twenties discovered it. The rest of it has changed much more. The profile of the world is different and so, in consequence, is the structure of life. This is what made me say in 1914, and again in a book which was published in 1921, that the generation was the fundamental concept of history. At that time no one else in Europe was talking of this. A few years ago an historian of art, Pinder, using as a springboard those paragraphs of mine which he praised unduly but did not understand very well, published his book on *Das Problem der Generationem in der Kunstgeschichte Europas*, which first focused the attention of historians on the matter. (All the hints which had appeared earlier, except for the confused and self-defeating book by Ottokar Lorenz, and the relatively unknown one of Drommel, which I cited, both appearing in the previous century, were very slight, consisting only of a few lines and at times only a few words.) So I believe that I have contributed to the formal and considered initiation of this method of the generations, although, out of that indolence which leads me to talk about things and not publish them, I have waited until this book to expound my idea to the full.

As I was saying, Pinder, in spite of his favorable recognition of this idea, did not understand its essence. This is not his fault, for the paragraphs which he could read in the German translation of one of my books did not develop the thought sufficiently. But what I do not understand is why he should miss in them the distinction between contemporaries and coevals when this is the key to the very paragraphs which he quotes. In contrast to all the other theories on the generations, and even to the very old and traditional idea about them, I take them not as a succession, but as a polemic (always taking this word seriously and not in a frivolous sense as the young use it these days), a controversy, an argument. This does not, of course, mean that the life of each generation consists of struggling against the previous generation, which is what youth in these last fifteen years has believed—thus committing a much greater error than they suspect, and one having very deep roots, which will bring catastrophic consequences—catastrophic for them, that is, because those who are not young no longer suffer catastrophes. This controversy is not necessarily negative in character; on the contrary, the essential argument between the generations has in normal history the form of, or better, it is *formally* sequence, education, collaboration, and the prolongation of the previous by the subsequent.

So I am saying that until now the idea of the generations has been more or less confused with genealogy, with the biological series—one might better say zoological—of sons, fathers, and grandfathers. All the primitive histories, the Hebraic, for example, are constructed on the thread of genealogies.

Thus the gospel according to St. Matthew begins with these words: "The book of the generation of Jesus Christ, the son of David, the son of Abraham. Abraham begat Isaac; and Isaac begat Jacob; and Jacob begat Judas and his brethren"; and so on. In this fashion the primitive historians placed Jesus on a specific level of general human destiny as measured by genealogical generations. This reveals a shrewd intuition that the life of man is fitted into a broader process, within which it represents a stage. The individual is ascribed to his generation; the generation is not just anywhere, Utopian and timeless, but set between two specific generations. Just as in our individual lives the thing we are now doing, and therefore the person we now are, occupies an irretrievable sector of the specific time which our existence is going to endure, so each generation represents an essential, irretrievable and not to be transferred bit of historic time, of the vital trajectory of humanity.

This is what makes man a part of the substance of history; this is why I told you in the first chapter that life is the opposite of the Utopian and the timeless—it is the having to be in a certain "here" and in a unique "now" for which there are no possible substitutes. The present of human destiny, the present in which we are living—or better, the present in which we have our being, understanding by that our individual lives—is what it is for the reason that on it rests the weight of all the other presents, all the other generations. If those presents which are now the past, if the structure of life in those generations, had been something else, our situation also would be different. In this sense each human generation carries within itself all the previous generations, and appears like a foreshortening of universal history. And in the same sense one must recognize that the past is here among us, that we are its summing up, that our present is made out of the material of that past, which past is therefore the moment at hand, the heart, the hidden core, of the present.

In principle, therefore, it does not matter whether one generation applauds the previous generation or hisses it —in either event, it carries the previous generation within itself. If the image were not so baroque, we might present the generations not horizontally but vertically, one on top of the other, like acrobats in the circus making a human tower. Rising one on the shoulders of another, he who is on top enjoys the sensation of dominating the rest; but he should also note that at the same time he is the prisoner of the others. This would serve to warn us that what has passed is not merely the past and nothing more, that we are not riding free in the air but standing on its shoulders, that we are in and of the past, a most definite past which continues the human trajectory up to the present moment, which could have been very different from what it was, but which, once having been, is irremediable—it is our present, in which, whether we like it or not, we thrash about like shipwrecked sailors.

Beneath the confusion which exists between the historic and the genealogical generations—those sons, fathers, grandfathers—there beats a sure recognition that the concept which expresses history's effective articulation is that of the generation, and that by the same token it is the generation which provides the fundamental method for historic investigation. And it is not strange that the only book which up to now has been seriously dedicated to the theme of the generations, that by Ottokar Lorenz, tumbles headlong into this confusion and expounds a genealogical theory which, as was inevitable, rendered the author's effort completely sterile.

If one interprets the generations in the genealogical sense one emphasizes in them only the factor of succession. Thus Homer, like the Bible and, I repeat, like all primitive history, compares them to the dry leaves which come off in the autumn to be replaced by other new ones in the spring. Succession, substitutions! All this stems from the fact that the concept of the generation is formed from the point of view of the individual, and focused according to a perspective which is subjective and familiar—that of sons, fathers, grandfathers. Such a concept is supported by an idea of ages which is also subjective and personal. By the word *youth* one understands a certain state of the body and soul of man which is very different from the state which both body and soul present in old age. But this assumes that man is primordially his body and soul. My entire thinking rebels against this error. Man is primarily his life—a certain span of years with its maximum length fixed in advance. And his age, as we saw in the previous chapter, is first of all a stage in that trajectory, and not a state of his body or his soul.

There are men who reach the end of a long existence with an uninterrupted bodily vigor which, taken by itself, would make it difficult to distinguish between the high tide of their youth, their maturity, and their old age. Among intellectuals the thing seems even clearer. For it is well known that the peak of intellectual life is reached when a man is around fifty. That age would be his mind's youth. But it is not that way. That man whose physical youth seems unfading, has, like any other, passed through the inexorable stages of existence; still young in body, he has had to live through maturity and then the life of an old man. And in fact Aristotle puts the *akme'*, or bodily flowering of man, between thirty and thirty-five; and the intellectual *akme'* (with an excess of precision which is not a little surprising) at fifty-one. With which, let it be said in passing, he reveals his own adherence to the perennial error, more serious in him than in anyone else, of believing that man is in substance the biological organism —body and soul—with which man lives.

The essential discovery that in man the substantive thing is his life, and that all the rest is adjectival to it, that man is drama, destiny, but not thing, gives us a sudden flash of illumination on this entire problem. The ages are ages of our lives and not primarily of our organisms— they are the different stages into which the things we do in life are segmented. Remember that life is no other thing than what we have to do and have to make, since we must make ourselves in making it. And each age constitutes a peculiar type of effort. In the first period man acquaints himself with the world into which he has fallen, in which he must live—this is childhood and all that part of bodily youth which reaches to the thirties. At this age man begins to react on his own account against the world which he has found; he invents new ideas about the world's problems—science, technology, religion, politics, industry, art, social customs. He himself, and others, make propaganda out of all that innovation, just as, vice versa, they integrate their creations with those of their coevals who, like them, are obliged to react against the world they found. And thus, one fine day, they find themselves with their world made over; the world which is their work has become the world in force. It is now the thing that is accepted, the thing that rules—in science, in politics, in art, and so on. At that moment a new stage in life begins. Man upholds a world which he has produced, he directs it, governs it, defends it. He defends it because some new men of thirty begin in their turn to react against this new ruling order.

This description shows clearly that so far as history is concerned there is one specific portion of our lives which is the most important. The boy and the old man hardly intervene in history, the former not yet, the latter no longer. But neither does man act a positive historic role in his first youth. His historic, his public, role is then passive. He learns in school and in various posts, he serves in the armed forces. For both the boy and the youth, active life is still on the threshold of the historic and concerned with personal affairs. Indeed this is the formidably egotistical stage of life. The young man lives for himself. He does not create things, he does not worry about collective life. He plays at creating things—for example, he entertains himself by publishing youth reviews—he plays at busying himself with problems of the collective type, and at times with such passion and such heroism that anyone ignorant of the secrets of human life would be led to believe that his preoccupation was genuine. But in truth, all this is a pretext for concerning himself with himself, and so that he may be occupied with self. He still lacks the substantial need to give himself over entirely to work, to dedicate himself, to stake his life seriously and profoundly on something which transcends himself, even though it be only the humble work of sustaining with his own life the life of a family.

So at any given moment historic reality is composed of the lives of men between thirty and sixty. And here comes the most important point of my doctrine. That stage between thirty and sixty, that period of man's full historic activity, has always been considered as a single generation, as a type of life which is homogeneous. This idea stems from the distorted point of view which makes one see in the series of generations only the elements of succession and substitution.

Let us correct this astigmatism.

Let us start from the man in his thirties who is, for example, busy with science. At that age he has learned the amount of science that is already in existence, has installed himself within the ruling scientific world. But who is it that upholds and carries the burden of that ruling state of science? Undoubtedly the men between forty-five and sixty. These men represent the knowledge which is already established, that which is there to go on being received, and which he, the man of thirty, was the first to assimilate. From thirty to forty-five runs the stage in which a man normally finds all his ideas, the first principles, at least, of that ideology which he is to make his own. After forty-five he devotes himself to the full development of the inspirations he has had between thirty and forty-five.

The same thing happens in politics: between thirty and forty-five man fights for certain public ideals, new laws, new institutions; and he struggles against those in power, who are usually individuals between forty-five and sixty.

The same thing happens in art.

Well, then, does not the same thing happen in a field which is historically more important than has been believed up to now, the study of which must be integrated with the new history? I refer to the basic dimension of human life in which the decisive influence is that other great elemental fact of humanity which, together with the fact of age, articulates life: sexual difference and its dynamism in the form of love. The stage in which man is truly interested in woman runs from thirty to forty-five. How, and why, are indiscreet questions for whose answering I would need an entire course—a course which surely must be given some day, and not in any casual place, but in a university, for it treats of one of the most serious and profound themes of human life and its history. Ah, that was all we lacked! Up to now, in talking of history and of the generations, we seemed to talk solely of males, as if women, and there certainly are a few of them, did not exist; as if they did not intervene in history, or had withheld their intervention for thousands and thousands of years until the electoral vote should be conceded to them. And, as a matter of fact, the history which has been written up to now is, in substance, the history of men alone—like certain spectacles which are advertised "for men only." But the fact is that the most effective, permanent, genuine, and fundamental intervention of women in history is found in this dimension of the love affair. This gives us reason to note in passing—and the fact confirms our idea that the word "generation" does not necessarily imply an identity of natal dates—that the women of any one generation are constitutionally, and not merely by chance, a little younger than the men of that same generation, a datum which is more important than it may seem at first sight.

But let us go back to the most urgent point of this exposition.

We see that historic reality in its fullest sense is carried by men who are in two different stages of life, each one about fifteen years long: from thirty to forty-five is the period of gestation, or creation and conflict; from forty-five to sixty, the stage of dominance and command. Men in this latter period live installed in the world which has been made; those in the former stage are still making the world. There is not room enough for two sets of vital undertakings, two very different structures of life. These are two generations, and—a paradoxical thing for old ideas on this subject—the essential element in these two generations is that both have their hands on historical reality at the same time—so much so that those hands are placed one above the other in formal or potential struggle. Therefore the essential thing is not that they succeed each other, but on the contrary, that they live together and are contemporaries, though not coevals. So let me make this correction to the whole past series of meditations on this matter; the decisive thing in the life of the generations is not that they follow each other but that they overlap or are, so to speak, spliced together. Always there are two generations active at the same time, in the full surge of activity, working on the same themes and concerned with the same things—but with a different index of age and therefore with a different meaning.

And the elders of sixty, have they no longer a part to play in that historic reality? Certainly they have, but a very subtle one. It is sufficient to note that compared with other age groups the elders of sixty years are very few in number—in this sense their very existence is somewhat exceptional. So also is their intervention in history. The old man is, in essence, a survivor; and he acts, when he acts, as a survivor. Sometimes, because his is an unusual case of spiritual freshness, he goes on creating new ideas or an effective defense of those which are already established. Other times, and this is more normal, one seeks out an old man for the very reason that he does not live in this life, he is in fact outside it, free from its struggles and passions. He is a survivor of a life which died fifteen years earlier. Thus it is that the men of thirty, who are struggling against the form of life which immediately followed that earlier form, frequently search out the old men so that they can secure their aid in combatting the dominant men. The gerusias, senates, and so on, in their primitive phases were groups on the margin of active life to which one went in search of counsel, precisely as though stepping outside of time, because those groups were no longer part of the full and effective historic reality.

According to this analysis, we have the fact that from the point of view which is important for history, man's life is divided into five ages of about fifteen years each —childhood, youth, initiation, dominance, and old age. The truly historic stage is found in the two mature ages —initiation and dominance. Hence I would say that an historic generation lives fifteen years of gestation and fifteen years of creation.

But in order to make the generation a rigorous tool of historic investigation we still lack one indispensable element, the clue as to how to decide exactly from which chronological date to which other date a generation extends. We know that a generation lasts fifteen years; but how do we divide the years which constitute historic time into groups of fifteen years?

As usual, the first thing which occurs to us is to start

from a private and personal perspective, each one for himself. Man always tends to make himself the center of the universe, and the more so when that man happens to be a Spaniard.

Such a young man who reads my book wants to know to which generation he belongs. Starting with himself, he finds three possibilities. Let us suppose that in 1933 this young man was thirty years old. As the generation, we said, is not a date but a zone of dates which we have now fixed as comprising fifteen years, this young man cannot know whether at his age, thirty years, he belongs to the fifteen years behind him or the fifteen years ahead of him; or whether he is in the middle of the zone which comprises a generation, with two groups of seven years each on either side of him. Or to put it another way, from the individual point of view man cannot be sure whether at his age date a generation is beginning or is ending, or whether that date marks the center of the generation.

Indirectly, this shows the objective character, historic and not personal, of the concept of the generation.

It is, as we have seen, essential to that concept that each generation springs up between two others, each of which is linked with another, and so on successively. That is to say, each generation inescapably involves the entire series of generations. Thus it follows that the determining of the zone of chronological dates which corresponds to a generation can only be done by determining the entire series.

How is this to be achieved? Here is the procedure which I propose to the historian.

Take a great historic ambit within which a change in human living has been brought about which is fundamental, visible, and unquestionable. That is to say, let us start from an historic moment in which man is living tranquilly installed in a certain type and kind of world. For example, in 1300—Dante's hour. If we cast a glance over the period which follows we will see clearly that with respect to his world European man was losing peace of mind. A little later we see that this world is going down, and that man does not know how to keep his balance. We follow down the years and reach another date at which we find him newly tranquil. He has set himself up again in a world which is certain, and in it he perseveres quietly for centuries. This panorama touches three periods: the Middle Ages, which lasted in full bloom until 1350; the modern age, which was lived to the full from 1650 on; and a period between them which is an era of indecision.

For the moment the Middle Ages do not interest us, and we take them merely as a point of reference. The period of indecision, being indecisive in character, does not allow us a footing for any firm conclusion. The modern age, on the other hand, shows us with ample clarity an insistent and continuous development of certain principles of life which were defined for the first time at a certain date. That date is the decisive one in a series of dates which make up the modern age. A generation is then living which for the first time thinks the new thoughts with full clarity and in complete possession of their meaning; a generation which is neither still the precursor nor yet the follower. That I call the decisive generation.

In the field of philosophic thought and the high sciences to which I have reduced the theme of this book, there is no doubt as to when this new era reached its maturity. Its crucial years run from 1600 to 1650. Within this period let us try to isolate the decisive generation.

For this purpose one seeks the figure who most clearly represents the character of the period. In our case there seems no doubt that this man is Descartes. Very rarely has an innovator played that role so decisively and so fully; his work of innovation was mature in form, completely conscious of itself, perfect in formulation.

In him we have the eponym of the decisive generation; having found him, the rest is a matter of mathematics. Let us note the date in which Descartes ended his thirtieth year—1626. That will be the key date in Descartes' generation, a point of departure from which the others can be fixed on either side merely by adding or subtracting groups of fifteen years. Thus the key date of the previous nearest generation is 1611, which is the generation of Hobbes and Hugo Grotius; then 1596, which, let us note in passing, is the generation of Galileo, of Kepler, and Bacon, a good little generation. Then 1581, which is the generation of Giordano Bruno, of Tycho Brahe, and of our Cervantes, Suarez, and Sanchez the skeptic; then 1566, the generation of Montaigne, of Jean Bodin; then 1551, a generation without great figures. It is not obligatory for a generation to have great men. Human life is not more nor less real, it does not cease to have its own exclusive character merely because it happens to be illustrious or mediocre.

But how can we group those names into generations if they were born in different years? The dates 1626, 1611, 1596, and so on, I have called the dates of generations, not of persons. Only in the first instance did we choose, as the date of a generation, the date on which one specific man reached his thirtieth year. Starting from 1626, we said that this date is the center of the zone of dates which corresponds to the decisive generation. Therefore, those who were then in their thirties belong to that generation, whether they reached their thirtieth birthday seven years before or seven years after that date. For example, the philosopher Hobbes was born in 1588. He was thirty years old in 1618. His thirtieth birthday was eight years before the thirtieth birthday of Descartes. Thus he borders on Descartes' generation—one year less, and he would belong to it. But mathematics, an automatic process, makes us put him, for the moment, in an earlier one.

What are we trying to do with all of this? Do we pretend that mathematical automatism with its characteristic stupidity and abstraction can decide a matter of historic reality? To a certain extent it can. That exact series of the generations serves us as a framework with which we can approach historic facts to see if they will tolerate being ordered and adjusted within it. Imagine for a moment that it is not this way; that Hobbes, when compared with Descartes, appears to be representing the same vital structure as Descartes, to be facing the world's intellectual problems on exactly the same level as Descartes. Then our series would be wrongly put together: we would have to correct the entire series, backwards and forwards, until the articulation of the dates coincides with the actual historic articulation, and Hobbes is brought to belong to the same generation as Descartes.

As a matter of fact, the case of Hobbes confirms the proposed seriation in the most rigorous manner. The automatic working of mathematics hints that Hobbes belongs to another generation, but that he represents the borderline which verges on the Cartesian mode of thinking. A study of his work, an analysis of the general attitude with which he approaches problems, coincides exactly with this forecast. Hobbes comes almost to the point of seeing things as Descartes saw them; but that "almost" is symptomatic. His distance from Descartes is minimal, and in all matters the same. It is not that he coincides with Descartes at one point and differs at another. No: in order to define the very curious relation between them we would say that they coincide a bit in everything, and in everything they differ a bit—as if two men were looking at the same landscape, but one was sitting some distance higher than the other. This is, then, a matter of difference in the relative height of one's position. It is that difference in the vital level which I call a generation.

To take a random example: from the moment that democracy came into existence each generation has been forced to see its problems from a different level. The experience of democracy possessed by the generation which started it cannot be the same as that of the following generation which received it from them, and so on forward. Even though they all live within the democratic horizon and in the democratic faith, their attitude with respect to it must be different.

If all this be true, it is not we who, by virtue of our immediate impressions, are able to judge to which historic generation we belong. It is history which, by constructing past reality up to the very moment of our present, establishes the actual and effective series of the generations. Such a task is by no means completed; it has not even been begun. It is this which, in my judgment, the new science of history is going to undertake.

The only thing of which we can avail ourselves, in trying to establish the concept of our time, is the general principle that the face of the world changes every fifteen years. In his biography of Agricola, Tacitus uses a phrase which until now has not seemed really clear, an enigmatic phrase: *per quindecim annos, grande mortalis aevi spatium*. That is: "for fifteen years, a very important period in the life of man." And he does not say this in passing, but in a paragraph in which he is considering the vital trajectory of the individual and of the changes in history. I think that this phrase is now clarified.

Accepting the presumption that the tone of history changes every fifteen years, let us now try to orient ourselves in our own period and to reach approximate diagnoses, always aiming at what in the last instance determines the scientific construction which only history can achieve.

With all this caution, these exceptions, these reservations, which give my work only the value of an uncertain suspicion, I would dare to suggest, by virtue of many, many reasons which I have no time now to list, that in 1917 there began a generation, a type of life which, in all its essentials, would have come to an end in 1932. It would not be difficult to sketch the physiognomy of that existence which coincided with the period called—and in my judgment badly called—"postwar." I am not even going to clear the ground for this subject. But if anyone is interested in a certain vital mode—a certain way of thinking in physics or in philosophy, or a certain fashion in artistic styles, certain political movements—and wishes to orient himself with regard to their future, he might well fix the date of its origin and place it in relation to 1917. For example, it is most curious that on that exact date the political forms called "fascism" and "bolshevism" broke out their first buds. In that year pictorial cubism began, and the poetry which is related to it, and so on. Does this oblige one to suspect that all this is already an inexorable part of the past? That is what we will be finding out, irrefutably, in the next fifteen years on which we are now embarked.

5

Again the Concept
of the Generation

In the previous chapter I finished expounding the first of the themes which I wished to advance in regard to the generations that are decisive in European thought; the generations from 1550 to 1650 which have as their focal point, both in time and in content, the work of Galileo. It was natural that that first theme should be the concept of the generation, which is, as we have seen, the visual device through which historical reality, vibrant and genuine, is made visible. At any given moment a generation is one and the same thing as the structure of human life. One cannot attempt to know what actually happened on such and such a date without first finding out to which generation this occurred, that is, within what framework of human existence it took place.

The same event happening to two different generations is a reality of life and therefore completely different in history. The fact of a war may have the most diverse meanings, depending on the date at which it occurs, because man draws from it the most contradictory consequences. This is why it has been so serious an error to lay hold on World War I as a means of explaining the profound changes which have befallen humanity. An isolated fact, although of the most enormous size, does not explain any historical reality; it must first be fitted into the whole framework of a type of human life. The rest is a chronicle's dead data.

History is the attempt to give the past new life, to live again in the imagination that which used to be. History must cease to be a museum filled with mummies and make itself what it really is: an enthusiastic effort at resurrection. History is an illustrious war against death. Therefore it cannot be said that something has been truly told, that something has been made history, unless one has been taught to see it born in the eternal fountainhead from which it springs, in which every human thing which belongs to man's life has its sole reality. In this sense, I understand history as the task of tracing all data about the past back to their vital sources in order to be present at their births, in order to force them again to be born and to live anew; they must be put in *status nascens*, as if newborn. The energy which the historiographer's work demands is poorly justified if history does not lead us to transform all man's past into an immense and actual present, thus gigantically expanding our own effective now.

And the event which I would like to help you to understand by offering certain ideas—doubtless immature and badly expressed, but in which I have great faith—is no less than the greatest incident which ever happened to European man: that radical shift of position which he made around 1600 and from which a new form of life emerged, a new man, a modern man. But the idea of history which I have sketched in these chapters, and which I have just reiterated, implies that it is not possible fully to understand anything in the past without indirectly producing some illumination of our present and our future. Therefore, if while recognizing the defects in those ideas I continue to have great faith in them, it is because they not only clarify certain centuries of the past for us, but also because at the same time they make us penetrate into the hidden reality of our own time and permit us to touch, perhaps with a bit of terror, its trembling heart.

The great turnabout of 1600 was the result of a grave historical crisis which lasted for two centuries, and which was the most serious that contemporary peoples have ever experienced. I believe this to be a matter of enormous interest because we are now living in an era of intense crisis in which man, whether he likes it or not, must execute another great about-face. Why? Is it not obvious to suspect that the present crisis proceeds from the fact that the new posture adopted in 1600—the modern posture—has exhausted all its possibilities, has reached its farthest limits, and thereby has discovered its own limitations, its contradictions, its insufficiency? One of the things which can most help us, as they say, to "emerge from the crisis," to find a new orientation, and to decide on a new posture, is to turn our eyes back to that moment in which man found himself in a situation which was both similar and contrary Similar to ours because then, too, he had to "emerge from a crisis" and to abandon a position which was frayed and exhausted; contrary to ours because we now have to get out of the situation which he was then entering.

At that time a new man was born, a variety of our species unknown until that date and not to exist again: the modern man, who began by being the Cartesian man. And it is in itself curious to note that this Cartesian man was then perfectly aware of the fact that he was a new man, a man who was being born, or, which is the same thing, the man who was being reborn. Strictly speaking, before that new man could fully exist, he had to present himself to himself and even to seek a name for himself. Toward the end of the fourteenth century and throughout the fifteenth, men began to talk about "modernism."

In theology and philosophy at the universities, the *via antiqua* was distinguished from the *via moderna;* and *devotio moderna,* which triumphed around 1500, was opposed to the traditional religious exercises.

This presentiment that things are about to undergo a radical change before they actually do change should not surprise us, for it has always preceded the great historical mutations; also it is proof that such transformations are not imposed on humanity from without by the mere chance of external happenings, but emanate from interior modifications generated in the hidden recesses of man's soul. Some years ago I cried out to Gog and Magog that the face of history was going to change; I foresaw it, rather as one foresees a change in the weather. And this anticipation was not merely vague or generic, but was narrowed to the definite expectation of certain ideas and opinions. In 1911 I gave a lecture in the Ateneo of Madrid on mathematical thought. That was the moment of the undisputed reign of continualism, evolutionism, infinitism in mathematics, physics, biology, and history. Nevertheless I said at the time that in all those disciplines there would soon emerge a tendency toward discontinualism and the finite. My statement about the profound—and at that time incredible—political changes which were to come was no less exact.

But I do not wish to recall now what I said then. Men paid no attention to me then, nor would they now. In 1916 I wrote an essay which I called "Nothing Modern and Very Twentieth Century," a somewhat petulant and mannered phrase, no doubt—remember that I was then quite young—but it embodied a prediction which has turned out to be amply true. Later, in 1928, I gave a lecture in Buenos Aires. Remember that in 1928 the world seemed more secure than ever; it was the time of greatest faith in unlimited progress, the period of inflation and prosperity. There had already been great changes on the surface of life, but it was believed that the mutations and the crisis would limit themselves to what was already evident. I said: "Many, many years ago, I predicted this imminent and total transformation. It was in vain. I received only criticism; my foresight was attributed to an excessive desire for novelty. Facts with their muzzles have had to come to silence the detracting mouths. There it is, before us, a new life. . . . But no, it is not yet here. The change is going to be much more radical than what we see, and it is going to penetrate into strata of human life which are so deep that I, taught by past experience, am not disposed to tell all that I envision. It would be useless, it would terrify without convincing, and it would terrify because it would not be understood; or better, because it would be wrongly understood."

I speak now of myself as I might also speak of others. Long before Einstein discovered his first theory of relativity, and with it the new mathematics, everyone was postulating a theory of four-dimensional physics.

The stage of pure presentiment which precedes the actual appearance of the new man around 1600 was the period which has since been called with a confusing name, the Renaissance. In my opinion, we badly need a new definition and evaluation of this famous Renaissance. Our knowledge of historical reality has advanced a great deal since the time of Burckhardt, and his first approximation is not enough for us.

The truth is that man was not reborn until Galileo and Descartes. Everything earlier is pure trembling hope that he is going to be reborn. The genuine Renaissance which sprang from Galileo and Descartes is first and foremost a rebirth of clarity; whereas it must be said that the era which is officially known as the Renaissance was a period of the most formidable confusion—as are all periods of trembling uncertainty, including our own.

Confusion goes hand in hand with every period of crisis. Because what is called "crisis" is by definition no more than the transition which man makes from living attached to and leaning on one set of things to living attached to and leaning on another set of things. The transition comprises two severe operations: first, the letting go of that udder which has been nourishing our life —do not forget that our life always draws sustenance from an interpretation of the universe; and second, the preparing of the mind to take hold of the new udder; that is, getting oneself accustomed to another vital perspective, to seeing other things, to grasping hold of them. The European generations from 1350 to 1550 accomplished these two hard tasks. Those were two centuries in which European man seemed to live in a state of complete loss. Obviously there is no such thing. To be sure, they arrived at nothing firm and positive; but during those two centuries the subterranean foundations of the western mind which were going to make possible the new construction were being polarized in a new way. When that underground work was completed, around 1560, in the generation of Galileo, Kepler, and Bacon, history turned a sharp right angle, advanced day by day without loss of time; and around 1650, when Descartes died, it could be said that the new house, the cultural edifice in the new manner, stood completed. This consciousness of carrying on one's life in a new style, face to face with another ancient and traditional style, is what is meant by the word *modern*.

The so-called Renaissance was, for the moment, the attempt to let go of the traditional culture which, formed during the Middle Ages, had begun to stiffen and to

quench man's spontaneity. This has been repeated time
and time again throughout history; but that is no reason
why we should find it any the less strange that, like the
fox who submerges himself in the water so that all his
fleas gather on his muzzle and then frees himself of them
in one rapid sneeze, man must periodically shake himself
free of his own culture.

The explanation of this surprising phenomenon—and
the most surprising thing about it is its repeated appearance throughout the length of the better known sections
of the historical process—is the topic which will occupy
us as the second theme in this book. It is that phenomenon
which is called an *historical crisis*. And in the same way
that I succeeded earlier in making the concepts of life
and of the generation take on a precise and fruitful meaning, so would I like to try to give the concept of historical
crisis a precise meaning. Galileo plays an extremely important part in that crisis, and in order to understand
it we must clearly understand the argument of the drama
in which he plays that role. This requires some preparation, and to this preparation, to the fixing of certain ideas
which we will later see operating in every crisis, we will
dedicate this chapter.

And first of all, let us not lose our way. Looking backward, let us remember the steps we have taken, and manage to insert into their proper places the new steps which
we need. The subject of our inquiry is history. History,
we were saying, proposes to find out how human lives
have been lived. What is human is not man's body, nor
even his soul, but his life. The body is a thing, the soul
is also a thing; man is not a thing, but a drama—his life.
Man has to live with the body and soul which have fallen
to him by chance. The one and the other—body and soul
—are the apparatus nearest to him with which he has to
live, that is to say, with which he must exist in his sur-

roundings. In order to exist in the environment into which he has fallen, he must make the effort to maintain himself within it—he has always to be doing something. And the first thing he has to do is to decide what he is going to do. But in order to decide this, he must first frame a general interpretation of his surroundings, must formulate for himself a system of convictions about his environment; this he needs as a map so that he can move about among things and act on them.

Faced with things as they are, as he finds them in his surroundings, man does not know what to do because he does not know what, in regard to them, he can depend on; or, as it is usually put, he does not know what they are. Life is, for the time being, all insecurity, the feeling of being shipwrecked in a mysterious, strange, and frequently hostile element. One meets those things called illness, hunger, sorrow. Just to give them a name is to begin to interpret them; the name itself is a form of definition.

But one also encounters thunderbolts and fire, drought and torrential rain, earthquakes, the knife which another man thrusts into one's side; above all, one finds that to beloved individuals, to other men, a very strange thing happens very suddenly. They were here with us only a moment ago. That process of being here with us was not merely a matter of finding them near us in space, like the stones, the streams, the trees. No: it was a more fundamental being with us, a coexisting. I take note of a stone and manage not to trip against it, or else I make use of it by sitting down on it. But the stone takes no note of me. Also I take my neighbor into account as I do the stone; but unlike the stone, my neighbor also takes me into account. Not only does he exist for me, but I exist for him. This is a most peculiar coexistence because it is mutual:

when I see a stone, I see only a stone—but when I see my neighbor, another man, I not only see him, but also I see that he sees me—that is to say, in another man I always meet myself and myself is reflected in him. I am here and you are there. As the here and the there express spatial proximity, as they are together, we can say that as you are there and I am here, we are together. But we could say the same thing about this table and those benches; this table also is here and those benches are there—they also are together.

But the strange thing in our relationship, the thing which does not happen to the table and the benches or to both of them together, is that though I am here, I perceive without ceasing to be here that I am also there, in you; I note, in short, that I exist for you; and vice versa: you, motionless over there, are at the same time here, in me; you exist for me. This is obviously a form of being together in a much more essential sense and one very different from that of one bench being next to another. To the degree that I know that I am in you, my being, my presence, my existing, is fused with yours; and in that exact degree I feel that I do not stand alone, that within myself I am not alone, but that I am with you, that I have my being with you; in short, that I am accompanied or am in a society—my living is a living with. The reality that we call fellowship, companionship, society, can only exist between two objects which mutually exchange the fact of being, which are reciprocally the one or the other; that is, I accompany you or I am in fellowship with you to the degree that you feel that you exist for me, that you are present in me, that you fill a part of my being; in short, I accompany you, I live with you or in a social relationship with you to the degree that I am you. On the contrary, to the degree that I am not you, that you do not exist for me nor for any other fellow man, to that degree you are alone, you are in solitude, and not in a social relationship or a companionship.

What a tremendous theme, this, of the polarity or the contrast between solitude and society!

Without going deep into that question, which we will touch on at another time, you will recognize how difficult, how problematical, perhaps how Utopian is true fellowship or genuine society. Because you will recall that our life is the life of each and every one of us, it is what each of us has to make for himself: it is the sorrow that I must bear on my own account and that no one, strictly speaking, can share. I cannot hand over to another a bit of my toothache so that he can suffer in my place; much less can he decide for me what I am going to do and be. Nor can I—note this well, because it will be very important—nor can I charge another to think for me the thoughts which I must think; that is to say, I myself must hold my own convictions, I have to convince myself; and I cannot transfer to my neighbor the task of convincing himself in my place. All this that I am saying is a platitude as great as it is fruitful; namely, that my life is not transferable, that each one of us lives through himself alone—or, which is the same thing, that life *is* solitude, basic and essential solitude. And nevertheless, or perhaps for that very reason, there is in life an inexpressible eagerness for company, for society, for living together. For example, to take the simplest illustration in the field of thought, the wish to agree with others' opinions is native to us. When man has a problem, his first move is to ask others about it, so that they may tell us what they think about it. This is the living root of reading and of the fact that you have come to see what I have to say. We ask questions with the intention of agreeing with others, up to the point where, if we must disagree, we feel obliged to justify our difference in some special manner.

From the depth of this basic solitude which our life unalterably is, we are continually emerging with a no less fundamental desire for companionship and society. Every man wishes that he were the others and that the others were he. An entire series of dimensions of life is made up of passionate attempts to break through the solitude which is basic to being, and to fuse ourselves with others in a communal being. The most radical of these attempts to escape solitude is that famous condition of love. One person loves another to the degree that in addition to being what he is, he also wishes to be the other, to consolidate himself into the other's existence; and in fact one feels the other's being as inseparable, as though it were one with our own being. If the other is taken away from us, it is as though half of our being is taken away, that very half which seems most important to us. The lover who is left without his beloved finds himself in the paradoxical position of preferring that his own being had been taken away and the beloved's left. Therefore Shelley said to his love, "Beloved, you are my better self!"

Fathers, sons, friends, comrades, represent different degrees of relationship in the course of our lives in which we feel ourselves to be living in company.

But here we have—and now I am resuming the thread of this discourse—suddenly something very strange which is happening to the neighbor who was accompanying me. His body becomes immobile and rigid, as though turned to stone. I speak to him and he does not answer. Responding to me is the typical and essential act by which I perceive that I exist for my fellow man. Now he does not answer me: I have ceased to exist for him; therefore I am not in company with him any longer. And I discover with a shiver that so far as he is concerned, I am left alone. The fact of this impression in which we feel that a fellowship has vanished into thin air, and that my life, like an ebb tide, retreats from being a life with another and therefore a broader life into a life with myself alone, a state of being left alone by myself, is what we call death. But this name, please note, is a theory, an interpretation, an ideological reaction of ours to the fact—not theoretical, but dreadfully undeniable—of experiencing a new solitude. The idea of death which involves the whole of biology, psychology, and metaphysics explains to us, permits us to know what we can depend on with respect to this solitude which is all that is left to us from a companionship in which we had a place. And by a transposition which is very frequent in poetry, the romantic poet will say: "*Qué solos se quedan los muertos!*" "How lonely are the dead left!" as if it were the dead who are left alone by the living, whereas he who is left alone by the dead is the one who remains, who goes on living! Death, for the moment, is the solitude which remains out of a companionship which was; as though we were to say, out of fire, the ashes.

I have stopped at this point, in passing, for many reasons which will become clearer in the pages to come; but mainly so that it may serve you as an example of the primary relationship of man with the naked surroundings, made up of pure and ill-disposed enigmas, which force him to react by seeking an interpretation of them; in short, they force him to think, to form ideas, which are the tools *par excellence* with which he lives. The whole complex of these ideas make up the world, the horizon within which we live. But ordinarily we live installed, too safely installed, within the security of our habitual, inherited, topical ideas, until we become accustomed to taking them for reality itself; the result is that we do not understand even our own ideas, but think them *in vacuo*, without proof. Our ideas are reactions to a problem. If we do not live that problem, our concept of it, our interpretations of it, lack meaning and are in no way lively, full, and living ideas. And it was important for me to make this observation because it is the key to an understanding of historical crises.

Within that horizon of life, that world, and in view of it, we do what we do and we leave undone what we avoid doing; in short, we live. That vital horizon, that world, undergoes a certain change with each generation. I have maintained that that certain change is normal and inevitable: it makes of history a movement and a variation, a process and a change.

I cannot hope that you will now remember the exact words with which I set forth the kind of world change which is produced in each generation. Few though they were, they were perhaps sufficient at that time. But I must now clarify the matter a little further because it is going to be definitive.

The world change which each generation, willingly or not, effects in the normal course of events, is a change in the general tonality of the world. Whether its innovations are more or less profound in this or that set of problems is secondary, even to a certain extent indifferent, so far as world change is concerned. Let us suppose—I was saying—that many things change which are concrete and even important; we will say that there have been changes in the world. But this is very different from saying that the world has changed. If we compare today's horizon with that of no more than ten years ago—and I refer not particularly to the Spanish scene, but to the entire horizon— we will be forced to recognize that in no field have concrete things changed very much, that in most fields the change is imperceptible; and true though this be, nevertheless the world change has been fantastic.

Let us take an example which will show the difference expressed in my distinction between changing the world, and merely changing something *in* the world. It is an example in reverse—big, clear, central to the theme of this book—of a most basic and fundamental change which in itself does not represent the slightest world change.

If there ever was a profound innovation in the history of European thought, it is certainly that which Copernicus brought about. Not only did this inversion turn the traditional interpretation inside out, but the object affected by it was no less than the entire physical world. The example, then, is unsurpassable. Well then, the work of Copernicus, *De revolutionibus orbium coelestium*, was published in 1543. What effect did it have? Did it transform man's vision of the universe? Not at all. His invention is concerned with astronomy; and although astronomy is the most important science for an interpretation of the cosmos, it is, after all, not the interpretation itself, but only a science. This is not to say that Copernicus' book passed unnoticed; every astronomer in Europe used it for the relative precision of its metric data. Nevertheless only one of them, Reticus, accepted the Copernican theory. And one must leap ahead to 1573 to find another man who recognized it for what it was—an Englishman, Thomas Digges. In 1577, another German, Maestlin, came out in its favor. He was the teacher of Kepler. In 1585, Benedetti also spoke in favor of it, but with many reservations, vacillations, and cautions. One must go on to the great Giordano Bruno, that heroic and mighty friar, a kind of spiritual Hercules, a constant battler against monsters, in order to find someone in whose thought the Copernican theory appears transformed from the realm of a private discovery to that of a world change. Now then, by my count, Giordano Bruno is five generations away from Copernicus.

And up to 1584, when Bruno's *Cena delle ceneri* was published, what effect did Copernicus produce during those five generations in Italy, the country furthest advanced, the home of the famous Renaissance? Literally none. The work of one of the most learned scholars of that epoch, the German Ernest Walser, has recently been published, and in it I read: "I do not recall having met with a single allusion to Copernicus in the entire Italian Renaissance."

The good Padre Feijoo, writing, about 1750, the letters which follow his *Teatro Crítico*, said: "In Spain the declaration of the Roman Tribunal against the Copernicans was superfluous partly because at that time *nec se Copernicus est audivimus* [we had not even heard that there was a Copernicus]; partly because in the matter of doctrine (even in Philosophy and Astronomy) our country is as motionless as the terraqueous orb in the popular System."

Padre Feijoo judges by what Spain was in his own time; but it would be a mistake to believe that the Spain of other generations was like that. No; the condemnation of the Holy Office was not superfluous for Spain, nor is it certain that Copernicus had not even been heard of. If Feijoo had read the decree of condemnation of Copernicanism in 1616, he would have been surprised to find that it was issued against two books and a pamphlet. The two books are these: the *De revolutionibus orbium coelestium* by Copernicus himself, published in 1543; and a *Commentaria a Job* by Didacus Astunica, published in 1584, before Bruno's work appeared. Now then, Didacus Astunica is no other than Fray Diego Lopez de Zuñiga, a Spanish Augustinian monk, who appears to be the first man to subscribe to Copernicanism in all seriousness and with decision, and to have set the presses creaking in Toledo with the new and wonderful idea. Let this be recorded in honor of this little Celtiberian friar; and let this correction of Feijoo serve as a warning to anyone who does not distinguish between periods of time, that is to say between generations, and who does not suspect the incredible differences which exist between a people which has lost its style and that same people during the time when a generation is living in full form.

This example demonstrates in proportions which are almost startling the basic difference between a change in the vital horizon and any innovation of a private type, no matter how important it may be. Why is it that the discovery which Copernicus made could not directly and of itself change the world of his time? On the other hand, why did it, five generations later, become the great idea on which a radical mutation in the human horizon was based? Very simple: during the Middle Ages the individual sciences, therefore science as such, represented a kind of secondary knowledge; they were, we might say, a spiritual activity of the second class. It is not enough for something to appear true within the specialized vision of a science for it to become, without further ado, a conclusive truth, an active truth. In the last analysis only theology and philosophy are creators of faith on their own account.

Translating this well-known fact into our own terminology, let us say that during the Middle Ages and up to 1550 the sciences were not world-makers; just as today we may add, though with some element of exaggeration, that the technique of chess playing makes no new worlds. Consequently, in order that a single scientific discovery like the Copernican idea should produce an actual world change, it was necessary for men first to decide to acknowledge the fact that, generally speaking, scientific truth is truth of the first class, a creative truth. Only within that general change in the evaluation of the sciences could the Copernican theory radiate all the formidable and vital consequences which were pregnant within it.

Now then, the five generations from Copernicus to Galileo are precisely that many periods in the revindication of the sciences as such. That was their role, their task, and their achievement. One has only to cite one or two names in each generation for you to see them as steps in a continually ascending staircase: 1506, Copernicus; 1521, Luis Vives; 1536, Miguel Serveto; 1551, Petrus Ramus; 1566, Montaigne and Viète; 1581, Bruno, Tycho Brahe, and Napier, the discoverer of logarithms. After these three, Galileo and Kepler were at last possible; that is to say, the time had come for a genuine, positive science and the faith in it.

This shows that the perspective of life is different from the perspective of science. During the modern age, the two have been confused: this very confusion *is* the modern age. In it man makes science, pure reason, serve as a basis for the system of his convictions. He lives on science. This is why Taine observed that whereas in another age man received his dogmas from the Church councils, he now chooses to receive them from the Academy of Science. At first sight, nothing seems more logical and prudent. What can better give direction to our life than science? Are we to go back to theology?

The fact that this reasoning seems to us so effective only shows that we still have one foot in modernism. The exact purpose of this book is to make clear how it was that man came to have this ultimate faith in science, in pure reason. But as this becomes clear to us, we may discover that to confuse the perspective of science with the perspective of life has its inconveniences, that it creates a false perspective, just as did the acceptance of the religious, the theological, perspective as the vital perspective.

We will see that life does not tolerate being supplanted either by revealed faith or by pure reason. This is why the crisis of the Renaissance was produced—for this reason a new crisis, shadowy and enigmatic, has opened before us. Confronted with revelation, pure reason, science, rose in protest; faced with pure reason, life itself is today organizing itself, reclaiming its empire—that is to say, vital reason—because as we have seen, to live is to have no choice but to reason in the face of inexorable circumstances.

One can live without reasoning geometrically, physically, economically, or politically. All that is pure reason; and humanity has in fact lived for thousands of years without it, or with only the rudiments. This actual possibility of living without pure reason makes many modern men wish to rid themselves of the duty of reasoning, refuse with active disdain to use reason. And this, when one is faced with the bigotry of pure reason, of "culturalism," is not difficult. We will soon see that every crisis begins in this manner. The fifteenth century also started with a cynical refusal to use reason. It is curious that every crisis begins with a period of cynicism. And the first crisis of the western world, that of Greco-Roman history, begins by inventing and propagating cynicism. The phenomenon is one of desperate monotony and repetition. But when men find themselves happiest in that apparent —and so easy—liberation, so do they feel themselves most hopelessly prisoners of that other and irremediable reason; of that from which—whether you like it or not—it is impossible to escape because it is one and the same thing as living: vital reason.

6

Change and Crisis

It is my belief that the so-called Renaissance represents a great historical crisis. An historical crisis is a concept, or better, a predicament of history; thereby it is a fundamental form which the structure of human life is able to adopt. But the concepts which define this structure of human life are many because the dimensions of human life are many. So it is useful to make clear to which of those aspects the concept of crisis refers. It refers to the element of change in historical life. Crisis is a peculiar historical change. Which one?

Reviewing what has been said in previous chapters, we find two classes of vital historical change: first, when something changes in our world; second, when the world changes.

The latter, we saw, occurs normally in every generation. Now we ask ourselves what is special and particular about the type of world change that we call an historical crisis.

And now I shall anticipate my own reply, so that you may know what facts to take hold of and may clearly observe the path my thought is taking. An historical crisis is a world change which differs from the normal change as follows: the normal change is that the profile of the world which is valid for one generation is succeeded by another and slightly different profile. Yesterday's system of convictions gives way to today's, smoothly, without a break; this assumes that the skeleton framework of the world remains in force throughout that change, or is only slightly modified.

That is the normal. Well, then, an historical crisis occurs when the world change which is produced consists in this: the world, the system of convictions belonging to a previous generation, gives way to a vital state in which man remains without these convictions, and therefore without a world. Man returns to a state of not knowing what to do, for the reason that he returns to a state of actually not knowing what to think about the world. Therefore the change swells to a crisis and takes on the character of a catastrophe. The world change consists of the fact that the world in which man was living has collapsed, and, for the moment, of that alone. It is a change which begins by being negative and critical. One does not know what new thing to think—one only knows, or thinks he knows, that the traditional norms and ideas are false and inadmissible. One feels a profound disdain for everything, or almost everything, which was believed yesterday; but the truth is that there are no new positive beliefs with which to replace the traditional ones. Since that system of convictions, that world, was the map which permitted man to move within his environment with a certain security, and since he now lacks such a map, he again feels himself lost, at loose ends, without orientation. He moves from here to there without order or arrangement; he tries this side and then the other, but without complete convictions; he pretends to himself that he is convinced of this or that.

This last is very important. During periods of crisis, positions which are false or feigned are very common. Entire generations falsify themselves to themselves; that is to say, they wrap themselves up in artistic styles, in doctrines, in political movements which are insincere and which fill the lack of genuine convictions. When they get to be about forty years old, those generations become null and void, because at that age one can no longer live on fictions. One must set oneself within the truth.

In one of the first chapters I said that there is no such thing as what is usually called "a man without convictions." Whether you like it or not, to live is always to have convictions, to believe something about the world and about one's self. Now those convictions, those beliefs, can be negative. One of the most convinced men who ever trod the earth was Socrates, and Socrates was convinced only that he knew nothing. Well then, life as crisis is a condition in which man holds only negative convictions. This is a terrible situation. The negative conviction, the lack of feeling certain about anything important, prevents man from deciding with any precision, energy, confidence, or sincere enthusiasm what he is going to do. He cannot fit his life into anything, he cannot lodge it within a specific destiny. Everything he does, feels, thinks, and says will be decided and achieved without positive conviction— that is to say, without effectiveness; it will be only the ghost of any real doing, feeling, thinking, or saying; it will be a *vita minima*—a life emptied of itself, incompetent, unstable.

Since at heart he is not convinced of anything positive and therefore is not truly decided about anything, man and indeed the masses of men will move from white to black with the greatest of ease. During periods of crisis one does not really know what each man is because in point of fact he is not anything with any decisiveness; he is one thing today and another tomorrow. Imagine a person who, when in the country, completely loses his sense of direction. He will take a few steps in one direction, then a few more in another, perhaps the exact opposite. The world and our convictions about the world make up our sense of direction, orient us, give us the compass points which direct our actions. Crisis man has been left without a world, handed over to the chaos of pure circumstance, in a lamentable state of disorientation. Such a structure of life opens a wide margin for very diverse emotional tonalities as a mask for life; very diverse, but all belonging to the same negative type. On feeling himself lost, man may respond with skeptical frigidity, with anguish, or with desperation; and he will do many things, which though apparently heroic, do not in fact proceed from any real heroism but are deeds done in desperation. Or he will have a sense of fury, of madness, an appetite for vengeance, because of the emptiness of his life; these will drive him to enjoy brutally, cynically, whatever comes his way— flesh, luxury, power. Life takes on a bitter flavor—we will soon meet the acidity of Petrarch, the first man of the Renaissance.

But human existence abhors a vacuum. All about this state of negation, this absence of convictions, there begin to ferment certain obscure germs of a new set of positive tendencies. More than this, in order that man may stop believing in some things, there must be germinating in him a confused faith in others. This new faith, I repeat, although misty and imprecise as the first light of dawn, bursts intermittently from the negative surface of man's life in a time of crisis, and provides him with sudden joys and unstable enthusiasms which, by contrast with his usual humor, take on the appearance of orgiastic seizures. These new enthusiasms soon begin to stabilize themselves in some dimension of life, while the rest of life continues in the shadow of bitterness and resignation. It is curious to note that almost always the dimension of life in which the new faith begins to establish itself is art. Thus it happened in the Renaissance. Why? Let us leave the explanation to another day.

On the other hand we are now ready to attack the root

of the problem of why historical crises are produced. This cessation of belief in a world system which was previously accepted, this fact that man shakes off his traditional culture and stands clear of it—a thing, which, as I told you earlier, occurs again and again throughout history—this is the very event that demands explanation. Compared with this most pointed question, everything else is secondary. But in order to understand it we must again submerge ourselves in that theme on which we touched in an earlier chapter, the theme of solitude versus society, and analyze it in another form.

I said before that life is solitude, basically, fundamentally, solitude. By this I did not mean to express an opinion about life which was at all vague. This is something very simple, precise, and beyond question; a platitude, if you like, but one with consequences that are exceedingly fertile. Life is the life of each one of us; each of us has to go on living his own life by himself. Our aching tooth hurts us and only us. The problem that I have, the anguish I feel, are mine, and only mine. And I must think a thought which will solve a problem for me, and either cure my anguish or lessen its intensity. At every moment of the day I must decide what I am going to do the next moment; and no one can make this decision for me, or take my place in this.

But in order to make decisions about my existence, about what I will or will not do, I must have a repertoire of convictions, of opinions, about the world. I am the one who must have them, who must actually be convinced of them. In short, this is what life is; and as you notice, all this happens to me alone, and I, only I, must definitely handle it. In the final analysis, each one of us carries his own existence suspended in the hollow of his own hand.

Concerning the most important questions of reality, I

must have an opinion, a thought about them; on that opinion, on that thought, will depend the resolutions which I take, my line of conduct, my being. It is necessary, then, that those opinions be truly mine; that is, that I adopt them because I am fully convinced of them. This is possible only if I have thought them out from their very roots and they have come forth nourished and advanced by undeniable evidence. Now, nobody can give me this evidence ready made; it takes shape for me only when I analyze for myself the matter in question, when I take it to myself and form my own convictions about it. For me to have an opinion about something is merely a matter of knowing on what facts to rely to determine my own position in regard to the thing. Several possible ideas on a question may occur to me; but I must come to an agreement with myself in order to see which one of them it is that convinces me, which one is my *real* opinion. An opinion which I have formed for myself in this manner and which I base on my own evidence is truly mine; it contains what I truly and genuinely think about the matter, and therefore when I think thus I am in agreement with myself. I am myself. And the series of actions, of conduct, which that genuine opinion engenders and which it motivates will be genuinely my life, my real and authentic being.

Thinking that thought, living that life, man is set within himself, is centered [1] in himself. Nor is there any way of being what one actually is, except by withdrawing into oneself—that is, before acting, before expressing an opinion about anything, to stop for a moment, and in place of doing something or thinking the first thing that comes

[1] Ortega brought back to use, and perhaps over-used, the verb *ensimismarse*, which means to be centered in oneself, to be withdrawn, abstracted. He plays on and with it and its components in a fashion that is the despair of more than one translator. Tr.

into one's mind, to come strictly to an agreement with one's own self, to enter into one's self, to remain alone, and to decide what action or what opinion, among the many possible ones, is truly one's own. To be centered within oneself is the opposite of living harried and confused—leaving to things in our environment the right to decide our actions, to push us mechanically from one thing to another, to carry us along without rule or order. The man who is himself, who is centered in himself, is the man who, as they say, always has hold of himself—therefore does not let himself get out of hand, who does not let himself get away from himself, nor permit himself to be alienated or converted into what he is not.

The opposite of being one's self, of genuineness, of being within one's self at all times, is to be outside one's self, far away from one's self, in something other than one's own veritable being. The Spanish word *otro* (other) comes from the Latin *alter*. Well then, the opposite of being one's self or withdrawing into one's self is to be in a state of otherness,[1] to be shoved about and confused. And that which is other than myself is everything which surrounds me: the physical world, and also the world of other men, the social world. If I allow things around me or the opinions of others to influence me, I cease to be myself and I suffer otherness, alteration, confusion. The man in a state of otherness, outside himself, has lost his own genuine character and lives a false life.

Very often our life is that and nothing else—a falsification of itself, a supplanting of itself with something else. A great proportion of the thoughts with which we live are not thought out by us with the evidence in hand.

[1] *Alteración*, which has the dictionary meaning of alteration, tumult, confusion, is in Ortega's word-play the opposite of *ensimismarse*. His own account of its derivation as he uses it impels the translation *otherness*; but the sense of commotion, of disturbance should not be forgotten. Tr.

With some shame we recognize that the greater part of the things we say we do not understand very well; and if we ask ourselves why we say them, why we think them, we will observe that we say them only for this reason: that we have heard them said, that other people say them. We have never tried to rethink them on our own account, or to find the evidence for them. On the contrary, the reason we do not think about them is not that they are evident to us, but that other people say them. We have abandoned ourselves to other people and we live in a state of otherness, constantly deceiving and defrauding ourselves. We are afraid of our own life, which is synonymous with solitude, and we flee from it, from its genuine reality, from the effort it demands; we hide our own selves behind the selves of other people, we disguise ourselves behind society.

But this society is not the true companionship of which I spoke earlier. The warm companionship which love intends to be, for example, is an attempt to create a union between my solitude, the genuineness of my life, and that of another; it is the fusing of two solitudes as such into one solitude made up of two. But this society to which I yield myself is of another kind—this implies that I have previously renounced my own essential solitude, that I have dulled the edge of my own consciousness, blinded myself to its demands, that I am fleeing from it and from myself in order to make of myself "the others."

My opinions consist in repeating what I hear others say. But who is that "other," those "others," to whom I entrust the task of being me? Oh—no specific person! Who is it that says what "they say"? Who is the responsible subject of that social saying, the impersonal subject of "they say"? Ah—people! And "people" is not this person or that person—"people" is always someone else, not exactly this one or that one—it is the pure "other," the one who is nobody. "People" is an irresponsible "I," the "I" of society, the social "I." When I live on what "they say" and fill my life with it, I have replaced the I which I myself am in solitude with the mass "I"—I have made myself "people." Instead of living my own life, I am *de*living it by changing it to otherness.

This is how those two ways of life which can be described as solitude and society, the genuine I, authentic and responsible, and the irresponsible, social I, the crowd, the "people," appear to us today, in a new guise. And in fact our life comes and goes between the two ways; at any moment it is an equation between what we are on our own account—what we think, feel, do with complete genuineness—and what we are on account of people, of society.

When we say that the life of man, when he is "people," is a false life—and that therefore man wastes his powers, dehumanizes himself, and becomes less of a man—we do not mean to level against that life an external judgment of a kind that sets up values. We do not mean to say that life *ought* to be genuine, that only when man is centered in himself is he as he ought to be. We are not entering into moral dogmatisms. It is very easy to laugh at morals, at the old morality which offers itself, defenseless, against present-day insolence. We are not dealing with that type of morality. What we are saying is simply that life has a reality which is neither goodness nor meritoriousness, but pure and simple reality in the degree that it is genuine, that each man feels, thinks, and does what he and only he, in the most individual sense, must feel, think and do.

Would you care to tell me what reality there is in a thought that I think without actually thinking it myself? When I say mechanically that "two and two are four," when I think it and repeat it without the distinct vision, without the evidence, that two and two are four, I have not *lived* that thought; and during the time that I employed in pseudo-thinking it and pseudo-saying it, I set aside my real living, I pseudo-lived. And I say the same thing about anyone who is reading this without truly reading it; that is, who has picked up the book, not to read it in earnest, but because other people are reading it. This person has wasted an hour of his life, and his life—please note—has its hours numbered; each hour that he loses by not being himself, he "de-lives" out of his life, he fails to make real.

The contrast between withdrawal into one's self and otherness becomes clearer when one compares man with the animals. And in fact, I will confess to you that it was on a fine morning many years ago in front of the monkey cage in Retiro Park that I found the evidence for this important truth.[1]

There is no doubt that the most important mechanism in every animate being is attention. We are where we lend our attention. For that reason I have so often repeated: "Tell me to what you pay attention and I will tell you who you are." Well, then; standing in front of those monkeys in the Retiro, I observed that not for a single instant do they stop paying attention to their physical environment, the landscape around them. They are as alert to it as though obsessed by any change which might happen in their cosmic surroundings. I thought how terribly tiring it would be for a man to be so ceaselessly attentive to his surroundings, so held by them, so absorbed by them. Man's situation permits him to be more or less inattentive to what is going on outside in the landscape, in the world of things, and at times to turn the focus of his attention inward and direct it toward himself. This capacity, which seems so simple, is what makes man as

---

[1] See the author's essay *Ensimismamiento y Alteración*, recently reprinted as a chapter in the volume *Man And People*. Tr.

such possible. Thanks to it, he can turn his back on the outside, which is the landscape, get out of it, and go inside himself.

The animal is always outside; the animal is perpetually the other—he is landscape. He has no *chez soi*, no home, no inside—and therefore he does not have an "himself." When, in a material sense, the animal is permitted to disregard his surroundings, when he can cease to be the "other" and depart from the cosmic outside, he has no place into which to go, no house of his own, no retreat, no interior, which is separate and apart from the world; therefore, when the environment leaves him in peace and without otherness, the animal is nothing, he ceases to be, and goes to sleep, that is, he does away with his own being as an animate thing. When he exists, he exists in permanent otherness and in a state of constant dread and outrage. Seals sleep continuously for only a minute or a minute and a half; at the end of that time they open their eyes, look at the landscape to see if anything new is happening, and again submerge themselves in the non-being of slumber.

Man, on the other hand, is permitted to have his being not always outside himself, in the world; he is allowed to retire from the world and withdraw inside himself. Man makes the Retiro a non-outside, a non-world: he puts the monkeys into it and for the monkeys it is converted inexorably into a forest, a landscape, and a motive for otherness. Man is the animal withdrawn within himself, the animal in retirement.

Granted this, and without posing any questions that are more substantive, we can, by following the simple thread of changes in attention, trace in human history itself the curve of ups and downs which the humanization of man suffers. An excess of sudden dread, a period of many changes, plunges man back into nature, makes him an animal, that is, a barbarian. This was a very serious feature of the greatest crisis in history, at the end of the ancient world. Barbarity followed Roman culture in that very period which is perhaps the highest that humanity has yet achieved—the century of the Antonines in which an emperor with a beard in the Stoic style, Marcus Aurelius, the best man of his age, wrote a book entitled *For Himself* as a symbol that humanity was living on a pinnacle of immersion in self. We know today that that ferocious crisis was not simply an eruption of barbarians flooding over Roman culture, but that on the contrary, cultured men turned into barbarians. It took nine more centuries—from the third to the twelfth—for man to reorganize his environment in such a fashion that he could again remove his attention from it and again withdraw within himself.

It is not easy to doubt that the phenomenon of rebarbarization has repeatedly recurred throughout history. The symptom is not lacking in the Renaissance crisis, which was much deeper and more serious than the Roman one. What the generations immediately prior to mine—Burckhardt, Nietzsche, and so on—enthusiastically called "Renaissance man" was for the moment a rebarbarized man. The Thirty Years' War, which left the center of Europe destroyed for a century, was the basin into which the resurgence of that barbarism arising at the beginning of the sixteenth century overflowed. Read what that war was like in detail and you will see that nothing similar occurred in the Middle Ages. Cesare Borgia was the prototype of the new barbarian who suddenly bloomed in the midst of an old culture. He was the man of action. In history, as soon as the man of action puts in an appearance and is discussed and pampered, it means that a period of rebarbarization looms. Like the albatross on the eve of a storm, the man of action appears on the scene at the dawn of every crisis.

With what we have said previously, and what we have added to it in this chapter, we have the ingredients needed to draw up briefly a blueprint of crises which will be understandable to us. It looks like this: Culture is only the interpretation which man gives to his life, the series of more or less satisfactory solutions which he invents in order to handle his problems and the needs of his life. These include the material order of things as well as the so-called spiritual. When those solutions are created for genuine needs, they too are genuine solutions; they are concepts, evaluations, enthusiasms, styles of thought, of art, of law, which really emanate from the deep heart of man as he actually was in those first moments of that culture. But the creation of a repertory of cultural principles and norms brings with it an essential, and, strictly speaking, an irremediable, inconvenience. For the very reason that an effective solution has been created, for the very reason that "here it is," subsequent generations do *not* have to create it, but to inherit and develop it. Well, then; the inheritance which frees one from the effort of creation has the disadvantage of being an invitation to inertia. He who receives an idea from his forebears tends to save himself the effort of rethinking it and recreating it within *himself*. This recreation consists in nothing more than repeating the task of him who created the idea, that is, in adopting it only in view of the undeniable evidence with which it was imposed on him. He who creates an idea does not have the impression that it is any thought of his; but rather he seems to see reality itself in immediate contact with himself. There, then, are man and reality, both naked, one confronting the other with neither screen nor intermediary between them.

On the other hand, the man who does not create an idea but inherits it finds between things and his own person a preconceived idea which facilitates his relationship with things as would a ready-made recipe. He then will be inclined *not to ask himself* questions about things, not to feel genuine needs, since he has in hand a repertory of solutions before he feels the needs which call for these solutions. So that the man who is already heir to a cultural system accustoms himself progressively, generation after generation, to having no contact with basic problems, to feeling none of the needs which make up his life; and on the other hand, to using mental processes—concepts, evaluations, enthusiasms—for which he has no evidence because they were not born out of the depth of his own genuine self. He works and lives on top of a stratum of culture which came to him from the outside, on a system of alien opinions come to him from other personalities, from what is in the air, in the "period," in the "spirit of the times," in short, from a collective, conventional, irresponsible "I" which does not know why it thinks what it thinks, nor why it wants what it wants.

Every culture which has triumphed and succeeded turns into a topic and a phrase. A topic is an idea which is used not because it is evident, but because *people* say it. A phrase is that which is not thought out every time, but which is simply said, is repeated. Meanwhile, the consequences of those things which are already topics are ending, although their internal possibilities are being developed; in short, the culture, which in its origin, in its own moment of genuineness was simple, becomes complicated. This complicating of the inherited culture thickens the screen between each man's self and the things that surround him. Bit by bit his life becomes less his own and more the collective life. His individual, effective and always primitive "I" is replaced by the "I" which is "people," by the conventional, complicated, cultivated "I." The so-called cultivated man always appears in periods of a very advanced culture which are already made up of pure topics and phrases.

This is an inexorable process. Culture, the purest product of the live and the genuine, since it comes out of the fact that man feels with an awful anguish and a burning enthusiasm the relentless needs of which his life is made up, ends by becoming a falsification of that life. Man's genuine self is swallowed up by his cultured, conventional, social self. Every culture or every great phase of culture ends in man's socialization, and vice versa; socialization pulls man out of his life of solitude, which is his real and authentic life. Note that man's socialization, his absorption by the social self, appears not only at the end of cultural evolution, but also before culture begins. Primitive man is a socialized man without an individuality.

Those who believe that the socialization or the collectivization of man has only now been invented commit a grave error. This has always occurred when history falls into a crisis. It is the maximum degree of man's alienation or otherness. In every crisis it has been verified as starting from a different dimension. In the Roman Empire from the third century on, for example, under the policy of the Severi man was made morally and materially into a statistic. The intellectuals, who then customarily called themselves philosophers, were persecuted. The men of each town who were most individualistic and powerful were obliged to take the life of the city and especially its municipal duties on their own shoulders. This destroyed in spirit and in economic life the minorities which had created Roman splendor.

In the fourteenth century man disappeared beneath his social role. Everything was syndicates, guilds, corporations, states. Everybody wore the uniform of his office, even to the cut of his clothing. Everything was conventional form, preordained and settled; everything was ritual, and infinitely complicated.

Knowledge, for example, was presented in a form so intricate, so overloaded with distinctions, classifications, arguments, that there was no way in so overgrown a forest to discover the repertory of clear and simple ideas which truly orient man in his existence. I am surprised that there has been no proper emphasizing of the complexity of culture, per se, as one of the principal causes of the crisis suffered at the end of the Middle Ages. And as no one has taken account of it, no one has known what to make of the clearest and most continuous desire that was evident throughout the two centuries from the beginning of the fifteenth to the time of Descartes himself: the desire for simplification. But we will speak of all this in the next chapter.

Now we must fix on our general blueprint the point at which that cultivated man with an overloaded culture arrives; the fact is that he is found within that culture in a situation analogous to that in which the inaugurator of the culture found himself within his own spontaneous life. He is found smothered by his cultural environment as was the other by his cosmic environment. And the similarity of the situation forces him to a similar reaction. The man in the forest reacts to his problems by creating a culture. To that end he manages to retreat from the forest and withdraw into himself. There is no creation without withdrawal into one's self. Well, then; the man who is too cultivated and socialized, who is living on top of a culture which has already become false, is in urgent need of another culture, that is to say a culture which is genuine. But this can only start in the sincere and naked depths of his own personal self. Therefore he must go back to make contact with himself. But this cultivated self, the culture which he has received from without, and which is now decrepit and devoid of evidence, prevents him from doing this. That which seems so simple—to be one's self—becomes a terrible problem. Thanks to culture, man has gotten away from himself, separated himself from himself; culture intervenes between the real world and his real person. So he has no course other than to rise up against that culture, to shake himself free of it, to rid himself of it, to retreat from it, so that he may once more face the universe in the live flesh and return to living in very truth. Hence those periods of a "return to nature," that is to say, to what is natural in man, in contrast to what is cultivated or cultured in him. For example, the Renaissance; Rousseau and romanticism; and our entire period.

With this blueprint in mind we can return to the crisis of the years 1350 to 1650 and from that to their central moment, which was the Renaissance. Now we understand that man foresaw his own rebirth. He was searching for a new contact with his own self. But our understanding of that age is hampered by the external form which that return to himself and to nature took at the start, a return which, at first glance, consisted of a return to the classics.

7

Truth as Man in Harmony with Himself

In the last two chapters I have tried to sketch the schema of historical crises; that is, the general structure of life when one lives in the midst of crisis. Crisis, I said, is a division, a type of history, because it is a basic pattern taken by human existence. Classic age, golden age, are somewhat heavy names for the historical type which is the opposite of crisis. In the classic age, in the golden age, man believes he knows on what he can depend in regard to his surroundings: he has a system of convictions which are genuine and strong, a world before him which to him is transparent. Remember that in our terminology *world* means the whole body of solutions which man finds for the problems that his surroundings pose for him. Well, then; the world in which the man of the golden age finds himself contains a minimum of unresolved problems.

But if one wishes really to understand these formulae, all the concepts used in them must be referred to the basic reality which is our life; that is, they must be understood in a living sense. Today we tend to take these words *problem, solution*, in an intellectual sense, or rather in a scientific sense, as if *problem* meant only a scientific problem, and *solution* merely a scientific solution. That propensity simply reveals what our ruling world, the system of our convictions, is, or has been until recently. As a matter of fact, we live on science, that is, on our faith in science. And this faith is neither more nor less a faith than any other; by which, please note, I do not mean to say that it may not perhaps be better justified and in some sense superior to any other faith. All that I am saying is that what we are discussing is a faith; that science is a faith, a belief to which one subscribes just as one may subscribe to a religious belief.

The history with which we are going to deal concerns the transition which man makes from a state of subscribing to the belief that God is truth, to one of believing that truth is science, human reason; hence, the transition from Christianity to humanist rationalism. It is therefore very important for us to take a position which is sufficiently profound so that we can discern not only wherein the one belief differs from the other, but also what they have in common.

Therefore we must correct from the root up one of the most stubborn and insistent ideas in the whole long stretch of man's intellectual tradition—the idea that man is naturally inclined to knowledge. The expression is Aristotle's; but the thought is present in almost all philosophies, to the extent that, unlike Aristotle, they do not even take the trouble to make it clear. That thought is what leads to the definition of man as *homo sapiens*, as the all-wise animal, a definition which I asked you earlier to reject.

We cannot now try to develop this theme adequately, though it is undoubtedly fundamental in all philosophy. Reduced to its simplest form and expressed with laconic dogmatism, we have the following:

Almost all great philosophies have started from two suppositions: (1) Things, in addition to the part they play in their immediate relationship with us, have on their own account a second reality, hidden and more important than that which is immediate and apparent, a latent reality, which we call their self, their being. Thus this light, in addition to consisting of what I see and having the function of supplying me with light, has a self, an essence, a being as light. (2) Man must busy himself in discovering that being, that self, of things.

Incredible as it may seem, the philosophies of the past have not set for themselves the question—at least they have not done so very deeply—of whether these two suppositions are solid. They take it for granted that things have, in themselves, a being; and they begin without further ado to investigate what kind of a being it is. Some interpret it one way, others another; but all of them assume it as existent. In the same way they deem it the most natural action in the world, and one about which there is no room for discussion, that man should exert himself to find out about that self, that being, of things; this occupation is expressed by the words *to comprehend* and *to know*. And in almost all of the philosophies one feels the conviction that man is only properly and fully man when he is busied with knowing. According to this theory I must exert myself in order to know, to form for myself, as I confront each separate thing, a thought which reflects its being, thus making my thought coincide with the self, the being, of these things. When I have not succeeded in forging that thought for myself, I do not know what the thing is, and then the thing is a problem to me. Now, then; the number of things, whose self, whose being, I do not know is infinite, and furthermore, I have not even observed most of them. Nevertheless, according to this idea, they are still a problem to me, since I have no idea, no notion, of their selves.

In the face of such absurdity, one asks humbly of the philosopher: "But, Sir, why all this? Why should I not content myself with seeing this light and arranging it so that it illumines me when I need it, rather than having to wear myself out in pursuit of its supposed self, or, what is even worse, in pursuit of the supposed self of things which even as simple things are unknown to me, of whose very existence I have no knowledge? I do not need long explanations in order to understand that everything which touches me is of interest to me; and if I have a being, I understand that I ought to busy myself in discovering it. But, good heavens, is it as evident and clear that I must also concern myself with that being which, according to the philosophers, things have on their own account? Is this assumption not arbitrary? I see that there are certain men who busy themselves in ascertaining the inner being of certain things: the mathematician, the physicist, the biologist, the historian, the philosopher—these are the intellectuals. But I do not pretend to be anything but a poor man who found himself obliged to live without having been consulted before he was born. Why, then, have I any obligation to be an intellectual? In the whole of Greek thought, in almost all medieval and modern thought, there beats this assertion that to be a man is to be an intellectual. But, Sir, why? Give me a reason, though it be only a pretext, provided that it is a worthy pretext."

I do not see why I am obliged to concern myself with the nature of things if they have this self on their own account, separate and apart from me. More than that, it might be well for those fine gentlemen who are intellectuals to justify themselves for what they are; they should explain why they dedicate their lives to intellectual pursuits. For each and every man, his life is the only one he has; it is the basic reality, and therefore inexorably serious. Whether he likes it or not, every man must justify his occupation to himself. If he does this and not that, it is for a reason. It is no good assuming that dedicating oneself to intellectual pursuits does not need any justification, whereas dedicating oneself to chess or to drunkenness must be explained. That is purely arbitrary. It is no good saying that since things have a being, and man has the ability to discover it, it is natural for him to use that ability. Chess also has pieces and rules, and man has the ability to move the former in accordance with the latter; yet one does not define man as a chess-playing animal. Similarly it happens that I have legs to run with, yet I run very seldom; and right now, for example, it suits me better to be seated.

We see with amazement that in so basic and fundamental a question the great philosophies have proceeded with incredible lightness. To know, which in this context consists of making a question and a problem out of everything, has not made a question out of what its own meaning is, of why man belabors the idea of knowing, and worries himself about it. Is there not a strange intellectual prejudice here, especially strange because of the frequency and steadiness with which humanity has suffered it, with only brief interruptions, for twenty-seven or twenty-eight centuries?

I repeat my question: why must I concern myself with the formulation of thoughts which reflect the essential being of things? Out of curiosity? Science is in a bad way if it stems from a source so low and frivolous. The curious man is the one who busies himself in what is really no concern of his. Curiosity is almost, almost, the definition of frivolity itself. Seen in such a light, science would be at best a hobby, a taste, an inclination. But no one is obliged to have a specific hobby.

The positivists think they can explain why man busies himself with learning by saying that it is useful for him to know: when he ascertains the essence of things, he acquires a means of dominating them and exercising his rule over them. According to this view, knowledge has a utilitarian origin. A lucid explanation! In order to become aware that knowledge brings dominion over things, there must first be a knowledge which has been won without expectation of usefulness; once this is possessed one may note that it yields utility. How could the first man who dedicated himself to knowledge know the advantages which his occupation might bring him? And above all, how did he know, how did it occur to him, that things have a being?

Moreover, even if it turns out, as has always been believed, that things have a being on their own account, it would seem to me very difficult to justify man's having any interest in concerning himself with it. The contrary state of affairs would seem more likely. For it is possible that the truth is just the opposite of what has been assumed up to now: that things do *not* have a self of their own, and that for the very reason that they do not have it, man feels lost among them, stranded among them, and has no choice but to create a being for them, to invent one for their sake and for his own. If this should be the case, we would have the most appalling overturn of philosophic tradition imaginable. What! The being, the self—which seems to mean what is already here, what *already* is—this is to consist of something which has to be made, when man's life is so wearisome as it is, so laborious, so full of things to be done for the very reason that he must make his life as he goes along in it? Ah! then one would understand why the essence of things should be of interest to man, why man should concern himself in thinking about them in order to find this out. Because then things would not possess their beings on their own account, but would acquire them only when man finds himself face to face with them, obliged to get along with them, and, to this end, forced to formulate a program of conduct vis-à-vis each of them;

that is, he is obliged to find out what he can do with it, what he cannot do, what he can expect of it.

The fact is that with respect to the things in my surroundings I need to know on what I can rely. This is the true and original meaning of knowing: my knowing on what I can depend. Thus the self, the being, of things would be an expression of the kind and extent of my reliance on them. A God who always has things at his disposal, who may or may not have need of them, or who creates them *ad hoc* when he does need them, does not require them to have a self, a being. But as for me, I am preoccupied with existing in the moment to come, in the future, and in what may happen to me then. The present does not worry me because I already exist in it. The serious thing is the future. In order to be tranquil now in regard to the minute that is coming, I need to be sure, for example, that the earth which now sustains me is something which is here. On the other hand, the earth of the time to come, of the immediate future, is not here, is not a thing, but something which I must now invent, imagine, construct for myself in an intellectual schema—in a belief about it.

Once I know on what I can rely in regard to the earth, whatever be the content of my belief, even though the most pessimistic, I will feel at peace because I will adapt myself to what I believe to be inevitable. Man adapts himself to everything, to the best and the worst. To one thing only does he not adapt himself: to being not clear in his own mind concerning what he believes about things. For example, one of the beliefs which man may hold is the conviction that everything is doubtful, that he cannot positively discover that self of things which he so badly needs. Even in that extreme case man will feel at peace, and neither more nor less than when he enjoys beliefs which are more positive. In this sense, skepticism is a form of human life like any other. And nevertheless there is in it no room for thought to come to agreement with the positive self of things, since it denies the possibility of discovering such a self. What is essential is that the skeptic be fully convinced of his skepticism, that it be in fact his own genuine form of thought; in short, that when thinking this he be in agreement with himself and have no doubt with respect to what he can depend on when he comes face to face with things. The evil thing is for the skeptic to doubt that he doubts, because this means that he fails to know not only what things are, but what his own genuine thought is. And this, this is the only thing to which man does not adapt himself, the thing that the basic reality which is life does not tolerate.

But then *problem* and *solution* take on a meaning which is completely different from that which they customarily have, a meaning which in its origin excludes the interpretation offered by the intellectual and the scientist. Something is a problem to me not because I am ignorant about it, not because I have failed to fulfil my intellectual duties with regard to it; but when I search within myself and do not know what my genuine attitude toward it is, when among my thoughts about it I do not know which is truly mine, the one which I really believe, the one which is in full accord with me. And vice versa; *solution of a problem* does not necessarily mean the discovery of a scientific law, but only being clear with myself about the thing that was a problem to me, suddenly finding, among many ideas about it, one which I recognize as my actual and authentic attitude toward it. The essential, basic problem, and in this sense the only problem, is to fit myself in with myself, to be in agreement with myself, to find myself.

At the moment of coming alive I am thrown into a set

of surroundings, into a chaotic, stinging swarm of things; in them I lose myself, not because they are many and difficult and disagreeable, but because they take me out of myself, they make me someone else, they alter me, they confuse me, and I lose sight of myself. Then I do not know what it is that I really want or do not want, that I feel or do not feel, that I believe or do not believe. I lose myself *in* things because I lose *myself*. The solution, the salvation, is to find one's self, to get back into agreement with one's self, to be very clear about what one's sincere attitude is toward each and every thing. It does not matter what this attitude may be—wise or unlearned, positive or negative. What does matter is that each man should in each case think what he actually thinks. At best the humblest peasant is so clear about his actual convictions, so well coordinated within himself, so sure of what he thinks about the reduced catalogue of things which make up his environment, that he has hardly any problems. And the deep repose of his life amazes us, the dignified serenity with which he lets his fate flow on. There are very few of these countrymen left now; culture has reached them, and so has the topical, and that which we called socialization; and they are beginning to live on ideas received from the outside and to believe things they do not believe. Farewell to deep quietude, farewell to life enmeshed within itself, farewell to serenity, farewell to the genuine. As our slang puts it so acutely, take man away from his interests and you unhinge him, he is no longer in gear with himself.

For his part, the man who knows many things, the cultivated man, runs the risk of losing himself in the jungle of his own knowledge; and he ends up by not knowing what his own genuine knowledge is. We do not have to look very far; this is what happens to the modern average man. He has received so many thoughts that he does not know which of them are those he actually thinks, those he believes; and he becomes used to living on pseudo-beliefs, on commonplaces which at times are most ingenious and most intellectual, but which falsify his own existence. Hence the restlessness, the deep *otherness*, which so many modern lives carry in their secret selves. Hence the desolation, the emptiness, of so much personal destiny which struggles desperately to fill itself with one conviction or another without ever managing to convince itself. Yet salvation would be so easy! Although it would be necessary for modern man to do exactly the opposite of what he is doing. What is he doing? Well, insisting on convincing himself of that of which he is not convinced; he is feigning beliefs, and, in order to ease the pretense in which he lives, drugging himself with those attitudes which are easiest, most topical, most according to formula. Those attitudes are the radical ones.

I do not dwell on this because I want to speak about the present only as much as is strictly necessary for an understanding of the theme of this book, which is an historical theme, a vital episode in the human past.

May I sum up what I have said in sentences which are stripped and numbered so that they may fix themselves in your minds:

1. Man, whether he wants to or not, always subscribes to some genuine belief of his own concerning the things that make up his environment.

2. But at times he does not know or does not want to know which, among the many ideas that he can think, is the one that constitutes his own veritable belief.

3. The originating sense in which something becomes a problem for man has no intellectual character, much less a scientific character. On the contrary, because man finds himself and his life really lost among things and

in the face of things, he has no other choice but to formulate for himself a repertory of personal opinions, beliefs, or intimate attitudes with respect to them. To this end, he mobilizes his mental faculties and constructs a plan of the points of reliability which tells him how far he can depend on each thing and on the entire body of things which make up his universe. This design for confidence, so to speak, is what we call the self, the being, of things.

4. It follows that man is not born in order to dedicate his life to intellectual pursuits, but vice versa; immersed willy-nilly in the task of living, we have to exercise our intellects, to think, to have ideas about what surrounds us; but we must have them in truth, that is, have our own. Thus life is not to be lived for the sake of intelligence, science, culture, but the reverse; intelligence, science, culture have no other reality than that which accrues to them as tools for life. To believe the former is to fall into the intellectualist folly which, several times in history, has brought about the downfall of intelligence because it leaves intelligence without justification at the very moment of deifying it and asserting that it is the only thing which does not need justification. Thus intelligence is left in the air, rootless, at the mercy of two hostile forces: on the one hand, the bigotry of culture; on the other, insolence against culture. Throughout history a period of cultural bigotry has always been followed by one of anticultural insolence. At a later date we will see how these two ways of life—to be bigoted and to be insolent—are two false and unreal fashions of existence; or to put it another way, man cannot, even if he wishes to, be in truth bigoted or in truth insolent. And when he is one or the other, he is being what he does not truly wish to be. Man makes a play actor of himself.

On the other hand, our interpretation, by which we refuse to recognize intelligence as the end of life, makes of it unavoidably a tool of life, by the use of which life is rooted irrevocably in the vital sod and granted an imperishable existence. The traditional intellectualist maintained that man *ought* to think; but he recognized that in fact man can live without using his intelligence, that his understanding is narrow and limited. Our concept denies that intelligence, intellectuality, is one of man's duties. It contents itself with showing that in order to live man has to think, whether it pleases him or not. If he thinks badly, that is, without a sense of personal and intimate veracity, he lives badly, in pure anguish, full of problems and uneasiness. If he thinks well, he is well adjusted within himself; and that is the definition of happiness.

5. Therefore our real thoughts, our strong beliefs, are an inescapable element in our destiny. I mean by this that it is not in man's power to think and believe as he pleases. One can want to think otherwise than one really thinks, one can work faithfully to change an opinion and may even be successful. But what we cannot do is to confuse our desire to think in another way with the pretense that we are already thinking as we want to. One of the giants of the Renaissance, the strange Leonardo da Vinci, coined for all time the adage: "*Chi non puo quel che vuol, quel che puo voglia*"—He who cannot do what he wants, let him want what he can do.

6. None of the foregoing even touches on the question of whether the historical evolution of human life carries with itself a meaning such that man may come to have no genuine beliefs except those that are scientific— that is, whether man's ultimate genuineness is not reason itself. I cannot now enter upon so enormous a subject. It is enough for me to remind you that in fact man has

been coming through a period, beginning in 1600, during which he actually did not feel easy in himself, in his customary ways, did not feel himself on his hinges, so to speak, except when he thought in accordance with reason. That is to say, he did not genuinely believe except when he believed himself to be reasonable. Modern man, as I have said, started out by being the man of Galileo and the Cartesian man. Rationalism, having to think as a rationalist, whether he wanted to or not, was his fate. Will this type of man, this form of life which lives *on* reason, be definitive?

Describing certain phenomena of modern humanity in my book *The Revolt of the Masses*, I noted that there are beginning to rise on the European horizon groups of men who, however paradoxical it may seem to us, do not want to be right, to have reason. Is this a matter of phenomena that are superficial and passing, or is there coming into being a new type of man and of life disposed to live on unreason? Is there room in the human scheme of things, both formally and substantively, for unreason as a form of authenticity, or is it no more than a notorious symptom of crisis and of life lived falsely? Here is a gigantic question which holds within itself the future of all of us.

But I cannot allow myself to pursue this question. The matter to which I am committed calls me. Burdened with these discoveries as with optical apparatus, telescopes, spy glasses, let us go back to the beginning.

In the classic age, the golden age, the average man is encased within himself. He lives with an unequivocal repertory of sincere beliefs about his surroundings. His world is transparent, and contains a minimum of problems. Now we see clearly what this means. It does not mean that he has solved all those problems which are problems to us; much less does it mean he has solved all that the intellectual calls problems, that is, the infinite number of questions that the self, the soul, of things can give rise to. No. He has solved his own problems, that is, the greater and most serious portion of his own, of those which his own set of circumstances has posed to him. The same thing may be said of the solutions: they are solutions for him, he feels in accord with himself, he knows on what he can depend when facing the great themes of his existence. This perfect and admirable equilibrium between man and his surroundings which he achieves at such times gives his life those specific characteristics which we usually group under the name of classicism. But it is obvious how carefully one must tread when giving to the classic the value of a norm. Strictly speaking, only the classic is classic, that is, perfect, for itself. To wish that another era would live in the classic manner is to invite it to internal falsification. What seems profitable and exemplary about the classic age is not the particular content of its ideas, but the balance between them and its life, the congruence with which it habitually behaves. During the golden age, almost everything that glitters is real gold.

The Middle Ages had their golden age: the thirteenth century, the century which begins with Albertus Magnus and continues with Thomas Aquinas. Then man seemed to be installed in a world which was lacking in any great problematical gaps; a well-calked world where tragic and unsolvable problems did not intrude. Within that world, man knew on what he could depend in regard to everything around him and in regard to himself. He possessed a repertory of ideas that were clear and seldom complicated, yet complete enough so that all the worries of contemporary man could be foreseen—contemporary, that is, in the sense of belonging to that world. Saint Thomas went straight to the problems of his day without playing games or indulging in the heavy pleasures of the technician, of the intellectual. He moved to solve them because as a man he felt it was necessary that they be solved by the intellectual whom he carried within himself. Saint Thomas was not very acute. His gift was good sense. Duns Scotus was more acute and so were many others after him, notably Occam. But it is not man's highest mission to be acute; he is required simply to resolve his life loyally and sincerely. Saint Thomas did not allow the intellectual within him to play an intellectual's games, did not let himself be made a buffoon in his own image—he accepted as a man the obligation of intellectuality which his period imposed on him.

A great series of events had just befallen the West: madly, romantically, Europeans had invaded the Orient in the Crusades. The story of the Crusades has not yet been well told. They are one of the most extravagant things ever done on this planet. For the men and nations which undertook them, they were a calamity; but they had magnificent consequences for the men who were to come. The Europeans who went on them gained full contact with Arabian civilization, which at that time carried within itself what was left of the Greek; and when the remnants of the Crusaders came back to their western homelands, they brought with them Arabic-Hellenic science. A torrent of new knowledge overflowed Europe, Christian and mystical Europe, which had been almost purely religious and military, hardly intellectual, therefore very slightly scientific. This is the era in which the disturbing ideas of Aristotle gushed forth into medieval life in a current which represents science as such, reason stripped to the bone, and the exact opposite of religious faith.

Christianity then found itself facing this dilemma: whether to give battle to science by means of the religious intellect, or to consolidate faith with Aristotelian science; whether to destroy the enemy, or to swallow him whole. The first was impossible. By itself, the Christian intellect had not been able to make itself sufficiently strong to struggle with that marvelous force, the best intelligence of Greece. Only the second solution offered a way out; and Albertus Magnus and Saint Thomas adapted Christianity to Greek ideology.

This was the second Hellenization of the Christian spirit: the first, if one harks back to Saint Augustine, took place in its cradle. Christianity was born in the midst of Graeco-Roman culture. It is not easy to imagine two inspirations that are more antagonistic than the Christian and the Greek. Nevertheless the former had no choice but to adapt itself to the latter, adapt itself from its foundation up. In this respect historical Christianity has had a tragic destiny. It has never been able to speak its own language: in its theology—its talking to God—the *theos* is Christian and the *logos* predominantly Greek. And looking at these things sharply, one notes that the Greek logos is constantly and inevitably betraying the Christian intuition. To cite only a recent example, let anyone who is interested in the subject look up the book which Jean Guiton published a few years ago entitled *Le temps et l'eternité chez Plotin et Saint Augustin*. The Greek is blind to the other world, to the supernatural; the Christian is blind to this world, to nature. And the Christian has to make himself explain what he sees but cannot say to the Greek, who is blind to what the Christian sees. It is almost, almost, the familiar dialogue in which the blind man asks the cripple: "How are you getting ahead, my good man?" And the cripple answered: "As you see, friend!"

In these last few years, we are beginning to discover with some precision this perennial tragedy of Christianity, to which its material triumph may perhaps be due, but which has always shackled and impeded the spontaneous development of its inspiration. Without the Crusades, without Aristotle, there might have started in the thirteenth century the formation of a Christian philosophy in the strict sense of both words, with real strength. The medieval intellect was beginning to enjoy sufficient maturity for the task. But Averroës and Avicenna flung across the west the full weight of Aristotelian thought; and Albertus Magnus and Saint Thomas had no choice. Even at the cost of crushing a possible Christian philosophy, they had to impose on Gothic evangelical inspiration the deforming tyranny of Aristotelianism. This deformation is what Mr. Gilson in another very recent book, *L'esprit de la philosophie médiévale,* called Christian philosophy.

The true Christian philosophy would be an imaginary line which we can fix only at certain of its points: Saint Augustine, the Victorines, Duns Scotus, Eckhart, Nicolaus Cusanus. The fact that Albertus Magnus is now hailed as the inaugurator of Christian philosophy can perhaps be considered as one more act in the tragedy of Christianity, a strange *quid pro quo* like others that history sadly records. But be this as I have just described it or not, it is not a matter on which we can tarry. Our intention is to see how man abandons the medieval world, which in its deepest stratum is Christianity.

But, what is it to be Christian? What structure of life does the Christian way represent as opposed to the rationalist way of the modern age?

We cannot understand it if we do not first interpose a few, a very few, words about the situation in which man found himself in the first century before Christ. Greek man, Roman man, Jewish man, all of them found themselves in the same essential situation. What was this? Strictly speaking, one word describes it—desperation. One cannot understand Christianity unless one starts with this basic life of desperation.

8

In Transition from Christianity to Rationalism

WE do not know what is happening to us, and that is precisely the thing that is happening to us—the fact of not knowing what is happening to us. Modern man begins by being disoriented with respect to himself, *dépaysé;* he is outside of his own country, thrust into new circumstances which are like an unknown land. Such is always the vital sensation which besets man in periods of historical crisis. This disorientation, this onset of panic, this not knowing what is happening to us, looks very different to those of us who, having lived part of our life in a known territory, are fully aware of our own exile from it, from the way that it appears to young people who were born in the *terra incognita*. I cannot stop to describe these different aspects in which the selfsame reality, that of crisis, appears to the mature man and to the young man. The result is the same for both: the sensation of finding oneself at the dividing point of two forms of life, two worlds, two epochs. And as the new form of life has not yet ripened, is not yet what it is going to be, we can only search for some light in regard to it and to our future by turning back to look at the old form of life, at what we seem just to have abandoned.

For the very reason that we see it as finished, we see this old form of life with the utmost clarity. In reality it is only now that we have a clear idea of what we have called the "modern age." This always happens. Life is

an operation directed toward the future. From the beginning we live toward the future, and are aimed toward it.
But the future is in its very essence a problematical thing;
we cannot put down a footing in it, it has neither a
determined shape nor a definite profile. How can it, if
it does not yet exist? The future is always pluralistic;
it consists of all those things that can occur. And many
different things can happen, including some that are
completely contradictory. Hence the paradoxical condition, essential to our lives, that man has no way of
orientating himself in the future except to reflect on what
the past has been, the past whose form is unequivocally
fixed and unchangeable. So for the very reason that to
live is to feel oneself propelled toward the future, we
recoil from it as from a greased slide and fall back into
the past, where we dig in our heels so as to take a fresh
start toward the future, our future which we must bring
into being. The past is the only arsenal where we can
find the means of making our future real. We do not
remember for the sake of remembering. I have many
times insisted that nothing of what we do in our life is
done for its own sake. We remember the past *because* we
are awaiting the future.

Here you have the origin of history. Man makes history
because, faced with a future which is not in his hands,
he finds that the only thing he has, that he possesses, is
his past. Of this alone can he make use; this is the small
ship in which he sets sail toward the unquiet future that
lies ahead.

And this recoiling from the future to the past happens
to man all the time; in big things as well as in trivia. In
a little while, after finishing this chapter, when you find
yourself facing a future which consists of having to go
out of this room in which you read, there will arise in

you the memory of where to find the door by which you entered.

Thus the consciousness that we are going toward a future which is particularly problematical, toward a new form of life, sharpens our minds and awakens our interest in finding out how human life has been lived in the modern era. We see it today as a complete trajectory with its beginning in 1600 and its end close at hand. But this beginning is not clear to us if we do not take some account of how man lived in the era which came immediately before it. Then we note that the period from which modernity surged forth was a time of crisis like our own. Hence our very special interest in it. At that time, too, man saw himself forced to leave a world, a known country, in which he was living, the medieval world.

This is not simply a matter of there having been a modern life before ours, and a Renaissance before that, and before that a medieval existence. These are not a series which is merely successive, but a journey, each stage of which issues out of the previous one. If today we find ourselves with our surroundings gone sour, this is not by chance, but because modern life has been as it was, and modern life in its turn carried within itself as its heart the Renaissance, which was what it was because the Middle Ages lived as they lived, and so on successively backward. Our present situation is the result of the whole human past; in the same way, the last chapter of a novel cannot be understood if one has not read the earlier ones.

And it is very possible that one of the causes which produced the present serious disorientation with regard to himself in which man finds himself may be the fact that in the last four generations the average man, who knew so many things, knew nothing about history. I have noted many times that the type of man who in the eighteenth century or the seventeenth century corresponded to present-day average man knew much more history than man does now. At least, he knew Greek history and Roman history; and these two past ages served him as a base and gave his own present a long perspective. But today, the average man, because of his historical ignorance, finds himself almost like a primitive, almost like the original man; and hence—other things aside—the unexpected forms of barbarism and savagery which burst suddenly from his old and hypercivilized soul.

Let us not go round and round. The basic reality is our life and it is as it is, it has the structure which it has, because the previous forms of life were as they were in a very definite line of unique destiny. Therefore one age cannot be completely understood if all the others are not understood. Human destiny is a kind of melody in which each note takes on its musical meaning when it is placed in its proper position among all the others. Therefore the song of history can only be sung as a whole—as the life of a man can only be understood when it is recounted from its beginning to its end. *History is a system*—a linear system stretched across time. The series of the forms of human life that have existed are not, as a matter of fact, infinite—there is a certain number of them, as many as there are generations, a certain and precise and definite number of them which take each other's place one after another and grow one out of another like the figures in a kaleidoscope, forming, as I just said, a melody, the melody of universal human destiny. Because all other reality is included in human life, that life is *the* basic reality; and when a reality is *the* reality, the only one properly to be considered as such, it is obviously transcendent. This is why history—although recent generations have not believed this—is the superior science, the science of fundamental reality—history and not physics.

But now we must hasten to see what the framework of medieval life was in its classic hour. And we were noting that that life of the thirteenth century was the joining of Christian inspiration to the thoughts of Greece. Christianity is the basic and decisive stratum. And, although we knew that we could only dedicate a few dozen words to the subject, we were asking ourselves what it is to be Christian. That is, how—as an answer to what environment and situation—did Christian thought penetrate the human mind?

I have already anticipated the answer: In the first century before Christ, Greek man, Roman man, and Jewish man all found themselves in the same situation. As a book is made up of pages and matter is made up of atoms, so life—our life—is made up of situations. Situation—the word shows it—is that in which one is. And the place where man truly and ultimately always is, is in some situation. In respect to the earth on which I stand, I can be in very different situations. Thirty years ago I was in this same library, but it and I were in quite a different situation—personally and collectively—from that in which we find ourselves today. The true and definite ground on which one is becomes the vital situation. Thirty years ago, other Europeans and I were in a situation of basic satisfaction. What a pity not to have time to describe to you what that satisfaction was, and in it what aspects the world wore! Then we would see how dangerous it is for men to be too satisfied. Well, then; because the European was then in a state of such satisfaction, he is today in an atmosphere of worry and restlessness.

In a similar fashion the situation of Mediterranean man in the first century before Christ was one of desperation.

In order to make clear what that means, I shall recall
only one fact. The most representative man of that age
was the Roman, Cicero. In him was gathered all the
culture which was specifically Roman, all the juridico-
political tradition of the Republic as such. But triumphant
Rome had inevitably allowed itself to be contaminated by
Greek culture. Cicero had learned as much as could be
learned from Greece: philosophy, sciences, rhetoric.
Which was Cicero's world? On what convictions did he
base his life? With what solutions, what firm beliefs did
he confront the problems of his environment? Cicero
was nothing less than Pontifex. Well, then; if you read
his book *De deorum natura* you will find yourselves
surprised by the fact that this man, who was the Roman
Pontifex, when confronted with questions as important
for life as whether or not there are gods, and if there
are any, what they do, how they behave, if they concern
themselves with men—this man did not know what to
think. He knew and he expounded all the theories which
the Greek and Roman cultural past—above all the Greek
—had evolved about the gods. These are many, divergent,
and even contradictory: Plato and the Peripatetic School,
the Stoics, the Epicureans. Cicero *knew* all these theories;
but he found that none of those theories was genuinely
his own; that is to say, concerning the problem of whether
there are gods or not, the Pontifex did not know on what
he could rely. That is how it was!

Do you think that without knowing what to cling
to in regard to this, that, or the other thing—because the
same doubts haunted him in respect to political institutions—do you think that anyone can live that way? One
can *live*, that is obvious; but one lives as though lost,
in a prolonged and mortal anguish. From a world which
has turned itself back into pure problem—and man is

part of that world—one cannot hope for anything positive; the substance of that life is desperation. In his book
De finibus bonorum et malorum, Cicero declares this
in a limited and formal way with a few words which I
have never seen adequately emphasized: "We academi-
cians"—that is to say, he, Cicero, declares himself an
academician— "are in the desperate state of understanding"—desperate from too much knowing. His book *De
Republica*, in which he analyzes the situation of the
traditional institutions at that political moment, reveals
a similar attitude. Pontifex though he be, he does not
know whether or not there are gods; as Consul, that is
to say, ruler, he does not know what the State ought
to be. Rome's political creations are too complicated.
Because things go too well for him in Rome, he found-
ers in his own abundance. He is a man lost in his own
intellectual and political culture.

Hebraic life has always had a very different structure
from the Graeco-Roman. It stems from the Asiatic form
of existence—Sumeria, Akkad, Chaldea, Babylonia, Persia,
India. While in western man the norm—which is perhaps a bit childish—is to be satisfied and only from time
to time to fall like a child into sudden hopelessness, East-
ern man has always lived in a state of desperation. This
is his primary and normal attitude. Satisfaction to him
is always satisfaction with himself, with what he himself
is, with what he has, and what he enjoys; it is confidence
in his own being. The Greek puts his trust in his valor
and his inventive faculty—in his reason. The Roman has
confidence in his State, in his Army, in his bureaucracy,
in his judges; for him, to live is to rule, that is, to organ-
ize; he has a regimental idea of life. But Asian man dis-
trusts himself; in order to live, he builds on this distrust
as on basic supposition. Therefore he cannot live on his

own exclusive account; he needs a support, a power stronger than he is, whose protection he can claim, to whom he can commit his life. This power is God.

But Asiatic gods have very little in common with those of the Occident. Western divinities are no more than the superlative degree of natural reality—they are the maximum powers possible within nature. Between man and the mythological entities there is a difference which we can describe only as quantitative, and which permits continuity between the human and the divine. It is strange to observe Aristotle's indecision in regard to nature. In his treatise *De divinatione per somnum* he says nature is demoniacal, not divine. On the other hand, in the *Nichomachean Ethics*, he says that everything which is natural is somewhat divine. This indecision does not exist in Asiatic man. He thinks immediately of the divine in dialectical contraposition to the human and the natural. His expression of this idea is, obviously, impure at the root; because man's intellect begins everywhere by being corporeal, or if you wish it put more exactly, let us say that it begins with an inability to think anything without matter. But despite this defective conceptual tool, there always shines resplendent in the Asiatic intent— perhaps the thing is only problematical with respect to China—the tendency to think of God as something other than nature, as that which is transnatural or supernatural. The natural, and therefore the human, is a reality which is constitutionally faulty and insufficient—so much so that if isolated and left by itself it could not continue to exist and would have no reality. Man feels himself to be a crippled fragment of another complete and sufficient reality which is the divine. For anyone whose life is based on that conviction, existence consists of the unending reference of one's own deficient self to the divine ultrareality, which is the true reality. One lives on and out of God, on the relationship between man and God, not out of oneself.

Well, then; Jewish life belongs to this type of structure. The Hebrew people, and within this each Hebrew man, exists thanks to an alliance with God. All his natural and intramundane activity is impregnated with and carried over from this primary contractual relationship with God. In it he finds the security which his distrust of himself could never give him. The bad thing is that that alliance, that contract, implies on Jehovah's part an extremely hard condition: the law. In the *do ut des* (I give that you may give) of this supernatural contract, God is with the Hebrew man *if* the latter fulfils the law. The law is the program of man's duties—a clear, terribly clear and unequivocal, program which prescribes the performance of innumerable ritual acts. The law of God is to the Hebrew what reason is to the Greek, and the State to the Roman: it is his culture, the repertory of solutions for the problems of his life. But in the first century before Christ, the Jew despaired of being able to comply with his law, and he felt as lost in it as did Cicero in philosophy and politics.

If you now remember the schema of crisis, of all crises, to the explanation of which I devoted two chapters, you will recognize in these great occurrences of Mediterranean history what I pointed out as the cause and the start of every historical crisis. Primitive man, lost in his harsh elemental environment, reacts by creating a repertory of attitudes which represent to him the solutions of the problems posed by those surroundings: this repertory of solutions is culture. But this culture, on being received by later generations, becomes more and more complicated and loses more and more of its genuineness. It turns into affectation and a concern with the topical, into cultural narcissism and the dead letter. Man then loses himself again, becomes demoralized, not now in the primitive forest, but in the excessive vegetation of his own culture. As that culture advances and develops, it arrives inexorably at a certain stage in which three things happen. (1) The ideas about things and the norms of behavior of which culture consists become too complicated and overreach man's intellectual and moral ability. (Let it be said parenthetically that shortly before Cicero's day, Varro informs us that in his time there were 280 different opinions about what good is, what should be aspired to.) (2) Those ideas and those norms lose their vigor, their liveliness, and their obviousness for the man who must make use of them. (3) Culture is no longer distributed with organic spontaneity and precision among the social groups which are creating it and is therefore no longer in proportion to their understanding of and feeling for it; on the contrary, this higher culture is now injected mechanically, as it were, into the masses. These, on becoming cultured (by which one means pseudo-cultured), lose their own genuineness and are rendered false by the higher culture. This is the phenomenon of socialization—the reign of the commonplace—which penetrates into the poor man and dislodges his real and authentic self.

Well, then; all these traces appear, some fully, others in embryo, during the first century before Christ. Cultures mix one with another, and at the same time become vulgarized. Greek intellectualism penetrates into Roman voluntarism, rending it apart, setting it off like dynamite tamped into a cliff. The Oriental religions, which for centuries had pressed heavily against the fringes of Mediterranean civilization, take advantage of the loss of faith in that civilization which Greeks and the Romans are beginning to feel and flood the reaches of the western soul. In passing they load themselves with Greek in-

tellectualism and Roman regimentation; and Oriental
religion starts to turn itself into a science, into a soph-
istry, and at the same, into an empire, an organization, a
hierarchy, an administration—that is to say, into a
Church. The differences between nations and cultures
are leveled. From the Gauls to Mesopotamia life becomes uniform. It is strange that all historical crises produce at the start an age of uniformity, in which everything has in it a little bit of everything, and nothing
is boldly and solely something specific and definite.
Saint Paul is a Roman citizen (*civis romanus*) and at
the same time a bit of a Greek philosopher. Cicero had
already received Greek knowledge from the lips of
Posidonius, a Syrian of genius.

In all this I am referring to the first half of the first
century. Cicero was born in 106 B.C. and died in the year
46 B.C. I want you only to note that in that period the·
desperation of ancient man begins. But obviously that
desperation, which is a profound historical reality, has
its own history, its stages, its heights, and its depths.
In this first moment one glimpses the fact that it was already there, active in man's subconscious. But the man
who carries this desperation within himself, who lives
it, does not yet see it, does not recognize it as such. At
most he notices it in some sector of his life; he loses hope
in this or that, but not in himself. Man follows on foot
behind his own despairings; but he can revolt against
them and try to conquer them. The empire of the first
century—the period of the Antonines—seemed to have
achieved this; and in fact, for very broad social groups
in the Mediterranean basin the time meant a brief period
of happiness such as the human species has hardly ever
enjoyed before or since. Perhaps only some period of
Chinese history can be compared to this midday hour
which ancient man enjoyed under Trajan, Adrian, Pius

Antoninus, Marcus Aurelius. It is not being arbitrary to call this century the Spanish century; the emperors who created the new situation were Spanish, and moreover they and the whole ruling class—which was the most cultured bourgeoisie—had been educated by Seneca. For four or five generations the old culture revived in the warmth of a new Stoicism.

Then suddenly, as if to prove that that stage of happiness was in fact something marvelous, something extra and unreal, unstable of balance, lacking roots or deep foundations, there came suddenly, and without breath or pause, the deluge: the downfall and the ruin of the ancient world. This was the last attempt to restore man's trust in nature; by definition, this is what Stoicism means. (And therefore, when at the end of the Renaissance things become clear again and man's new faith in his natural gifts bubbles up, we see Stoicism unfailingly reappear. Montaigne and Bruno are stoics.) But that first century's reaction against the disaster ahead shows us that though he had not confessed to it himself, man had already felt himself lost.

Cicero had villas, valuable books, money, and above all, literary vanity and consular pride. Holding fast to all these little things, he could blind himself to his latent desperation. (There are these people who so arrange their lives that they feed themselves only on side dishes.)

The Jew also was upheld by the pride of his tradition; he does not easily renounce the belief that he belongs to a chosen people. The Pharisee clings to the law which kills him. Nevertheless, and do not forget it, he is the man who has always despaired of himself, up to the point where he lives on the hope of another, of the Messiah. He is in this life and in this world without actually being here, as happens to everyone who is awaiting something, and he is in fact already living in the time to come, in the longed-for future. Only a little earlier the air of Jerusalem was on fire, electrified with the pure magic of expectation. The people lived outside themselves, in a morrow which was thought to be imminent. He is coming, He is coming! Who? The other—the other who can do more than we, because he can do everything, he who makes us whole, who saves us, the Messiah, inaugurator of the kingdom. And the urgent plea, which sustained this future-pointed nation for thousands of years, sounded again with new vigor: *"Marana za!"* "Come, oh Lord, come" (an expression from which Spain came to call converted Jews *"marranos"*—that is to say, those of *marana za!*).

The upper classes continued to amuse themselves with enjoying the things which were left to them—ostentation, power, luxury. That is, they were no longer really living from the inside outward, but on external things which fate threw into their hands as we might throw a piece of bread to the animals between the bars of the zoo. At the same time the lower classes were beginning to feel the fermentation of new ideas.

For the first time in the ancient world a campaign of propaganda was waged among the masses as such. From the heights where society lived, one could see swarming about in their long cloaks a crowd of strange men, clad in ordinary sackcloth, with staff in hand and foodbag over the shoulder, who called the common people together and shouted at them. This is no fantasy of mine: In the pseudo-Clementine Homilies one finds: "Appearing before the people, he spoke to them in a loud voice." Who are these men? Seeing them from above one was quite justified in not differentiating between them; actually, they had many external and even internal characteristics in common. Those demagogic propagandists were philosophers—Cynics or semi-Stoics—they were priests of oriental religions. Half a century later this broad group from the lower depths of society was strengthened by a new breed: the Christian converts. In the radicalism of their speeches they all agree. They preach against the wealth of the rich, the pride of the powerful; they are against learned men, against the established culture, against complications of every type. In their minds, he is most right and of most value who knows nothing, who has nothing—the simple man, the poor man, the humble man, the churchless.

When we consider 1400, we find that then, too, the crisis begins with a similar phenomenon. (Except that the crisis of the Renaissance, as I have already said, is in substance much less deep and complete than the crisis of the ancient world.) When one despairs of any form of life, the first solution which always occurs, as though by mechanically dialectic impulse of the human mind, the most obvious, the simplest, is to turn all values inside out. If wealth does not give happiness, poverty will; if learning does not solve everything, then true wisdom will lie in ignorance. (Parallels occur in the fifteenth century: the "simples" and lay-brothers of the *devotio moderna,* of the *Imitatio Christi;* the "learned ignorance" of Cusanus, his praise of the idiot, that is to say, of the uninformed; *Moriae encomium,* by Erasmus. The last trace in the sixteenth century was the *Lode del asino,* Praise of the Ass, by Giordano Bruno.) If law and institutions do not make us happy, let us set our hopes on lawlessness and violence. (After 70 B.C. neither elections nor assemblies could be held normally in Rome because Caesar and his rich friends had financed the organization of shock troops made up of gladiators from the circus, slaves, and non-Latin people—Phrygians, Myceans, Greeks, Jews—almost none of them real Roman citizens. This last can be seen from Cicero's speech, *Pro*

Flaccio.) Finally one last reversal of values, less pub-
licized than the foregoing, but which was in fact effected:
If men have not succeeded, let us put our faith in women.
And the intervention of woman in public life, both
political and intellectual, occurred; that is, *religious* life
was about to begin.

In my opinion nothing better characterizes the situation in which Christianity was about to take root than
the fact emphasized above: from a certain height and a
certain distance the Cynic agitators and the Christian
converts could be mistaken one for the other.

This easy and purely mechanical dialectic, which consists in finding the new by merely stating the opposite
of what is customary, a procedure so easy that it is within
the reach of everyone, prepared simple souls and even
the superior ones to receive the great and genuine innovation which was Christianity. In passing, let us note
the fact that at the beginning of a crisis the mind takes to
the dialectic form. This form, which at its best provides a
fabric for most subtle thought, later becomes vulgarized,
as in our own time. But let us get back to what concerns
us.

When the attempt at the socialization of man which
was represented by the Roman Empire failed, the Empire
was despoiled of every objective and public principle
which might have held a promise of solution, which
might have given meaning to its life and served it as
a point of support. For with the failure of the State and
its social forms, science also failed in terms of any objective and public standards to which it could be referred.
Man felt himself completely lost, with nothing to hold
on to, and he fell back on the only thing left to him.
When everything around us has failed us, we realize
that in fact none of it constituted genuine reality, none
of it was the important, the decisive thing; the reality

which, underneath all the other apparent realities is left
for everyone of us, is his individual life. Then man comes
again to see that in the final analysis this is the problem
of his own destiny—highly individual and not to be
handed over to anyone else. This is the state of mind
which led men to the Christian solution. The problem
was no longer this thing or that, but the very life of each
man in its entirety. It is not that man was hungry, or
that he suffered from personal illness or political tyranny;
it is not that he failed to know what the stars are. The
problematical thing was the very self of the subject himself. And if the answer to a partial problem is called a
solution, the answer to this absolute problem of the
personal being is called salvation.

Desperation, of which this crisis consists, leads in an
early stage to exasperation; and history is filled with
exaggerated and extreme phenomena with which man
managed to stupefy and to inebriate himself. After exasperation comes a new calm: one accepts one's self and
realizes loyally that there is no hope, that to hope for
anything from one's self is to fail to understand reality
itself. This is how man discovered his basic nothingness.
And this, this very thing, is, according to Christianity,
salvation. Instead of believing that the natural man is
reasonably sufficient unto himself, that he sustains himself, one discovers that he consists solely of dependence,
that his being, his support, his reality, and his truth are
not in him, but outside his nature. In believing these
things man had been suffering an error of perspective.
He now sees that the most important matter for him,
his life, is not a natural matter, does not consist of coming and going or enjoying, crying or laughing, not even
of thinking. All that activity is merely a mask, a costume,
a *mise en scène* for the really vital matter, which is his

supernatural life, his argument with God. All intramundane arguments shrink to mere anecdotes in this primary discussion which man has with God. One would say that whatever we do and whatever happens to us—in a word, "this *life*"—is only a mask which hides from us our true and genuine reality, the reality we have in the absolute, in God. So that what had seemed real—nature and ourselves as part of it—now turns out to be unreal, pure phantasmagoria; and that which had seemed unreal—our concern with the absolute or God—that is the true reality.

This paradox, this complete inversion of perspective, is the basis of Christianity. The problems of natural man have no solution: to live, to be in the world, is perdition, constitutional and unchangeable. Man must be saved by the supernatural. This life can be cured only by the other life. The only thing which man can do by his own strength is negative; he can deny himself and deny the world, withdraw his attention from himself and from things; and thus freed of earthly weight, be absorbed by God.

This paradox was the thing essential to the structure of medieval life, because it brings with it a basic tendency to disentangle oneself from the natural world. For the Greek and the Roman, existence was the problem of relationships between man and surrounding nature, visible or invisible. But to medieval man the world is in itself the ultramundane and the supernatural. For the moment, man is left alone with God.

It is useful to remember that at one time—a time which lasted many centuries—man was immersed in this Christian belief and his living took on the characteristic of a supernatural task. The modern age—Galileo, Descartes—brought us back to nature; and it is hard for us to recreate in our minds that way of life which consisted of living from God outward. As to the Greeks, so now to us, it seems a paradox.

But Saint Paul was fully aware of the frenetic quality of this paradox, of the subversive fundamentalism which the Christian idea carried within itself. He did not preach the good new thing as a reasonable thing. To preach reasonable things at a time of crisis is to wish. No: he preached Christianity and recommended it for the very reason that it had all the look of madness and absurdity. This idea is no invention of mine, not something I am making up, but Saint Paul is—an extremist. In the First Epistle to the Corinthians, we read: "For the preaching of the Cross is to them that perish foolishness: but unto us which are saved it is the power of God." Here is how this man, writing to the Corinthians, turns the world upside down:

For it is written: I will destroy the wisdom of the wise, and will bring to nothing the understanding of the prudent.

Where is the wise? Where is the scribe? Where is the disputer of this world? hath not God made foolish the wisdom of this world?

For after that in the wisdom of God the world by wisdom knew not God, it pleased God by the foolishness of preaching to save them that believe.

For the Jews require a sign, and the Greeks seek after wisdom.

But we preach Christ crucified, unto the Jews a stumblingblock, and unto the Greeks foolishness.

But unto them which are called, both Jews and Greeks, we preach Christ, the power of God, and the wisdom of God.

Because the foolishness of God is wiser than men; and the weakness of God is stronger than men.

For ye see your calling, brethren, how that not many wise men after the flesh, not many mighty, not many noble, are called.

But God hath chosen the foolish things of the world to

confound the wise; and God hath chosen the weak things of the world to confound the things which are mighty;

And base things of the world, and things which are despised, hath God chosen, yea, and things which are not, to bring to nought things that are:

That no flesh should glory in his presence.

That according as it is written, He that glorieth, let him glory in the Lord.

It is good—from time to time—to remember the past, to remember that these things have been said. A high official of the Empire who heard these ideas of Saint Paul —what would he think? That he was a little subversive? Yet what he was preaching—Christianity—was, as the current phrase has it, society's strongest support.

9

On Extremism as a Form of Life

I SAID that in the structure of medieval life the basic stratum was Christianity, and that the basic stratum of Christianity, in turn, was the recognition of the nothingness of man and nature. This recognition was made possible by the fact that Mediterranean existence had fallen from a situation which was satisfactory to one which was desperate. I am eager that you understand what I mean by talking of *desperation;* for this is neither a vague phrase nor the psychological description of a feeling, but a word which in all strictness defines a form of life. It is evident that man can come to such a pass that, although he must do something in order to live—we know that living is the condition of having to do something—he finds no occupation which satisfies him; nor do the matters on his material and social horizon or the ideas on his intellectual horizon move him to anything which seems satisfactory. He will go on doing this or that; but he will do it like an automaton, without achieving any sense of solidarity between himself and his acts; these acts he considers valueless, of no account, without meaning. When this happens there surges up in him an unconquerable loathing of the world and of living, both of which seem to him to have a character which is purely negative.

And as a matter of fact, before Christianity was born, and most of all before Christians made it what it is, many men retired from the world to the deserts, or to some other form of solitude. The solution provided by this

retirement was only approximate. These men were trying to resolve the problem of living, that is, of treating
with things and with neighbors, by reducing contact to
a minimum. Nonetheless it is important to note that this
flight from the world and this loathing of living are not
Christian discoveries, but the opposite: the Christian
solution was found for the very reason that men were
retiring from the world, because the natural was so hate-
ful men *sought* the supernatural.

The withdrawal by man into a corner of the world is
an accurate symbol of the first stage of desperation. It
means that man, in effect, reduces life and the world to
a corner, to a single fragment of what it was formerly.
This is simplification in the face of desperation, in the
face of feeling lost in an excessive richness of life—all
that knowledge and none of it enough; all those appetites
and possible pleasures, but none of them full and complete; that too great piling up of necessary occupations,
but no one of them with meaning which is absolute or
satisfactory.

The unfortunate thing is that, though he may not confess it until later, he who has truly despaired feels this
quality of negativity extending throughout the entire
ambit of his life, with no single point in the whole span
where he can make himself secure. I am very sorry not
to have time now to set up a catalogue of those figures
who take their lives when they see before them only desperation. They are many, and at first sight contradictory
among themselves. But I must say something about this
matter before we can thoroughly understand the origins
of Christianity and of certain phenomena characteristic
of the fifteenth century as well as of our time.

But first of all I must state quite precisely that I did
not say earlier, nor do I now say, that our own period
is constitutionally one of desperation. What I say is that

it is a period of disorientation, nothing more. Now then, it is obvious that he who is disoriented, and *only* disoriented, hopes to orient himself. This, I think, is the situation in which all the cultured men of all the world now find themselves, and among them my readers. The theme of my book does not pretend to provide you with the orientation you seek; it merely propounds a definite question about the past. At the same time it serves as indispensable preparation for other books in which I may perhaps try very hard to bring you a firm orientation. But note that I recognize that many of you have not come to these pages as you might come to a science lesson, but are moved by a much more profound and genuine desire: you have come to see if you can manage to orient yourselves a bit better. And I in turn have bent my book to that aim as far as I could so that you may in fact find in it something, however little, of what you seek.

I say, then, that he who is merely disoriented hopes to orient himself. But insofar as he is disoriented, and not yet reoriented, he is despairing. Thus there is a factor of desperation in his situation, even though it is not substantive and constitutional but only accidental and secondary. The similarity between the despairing and the disoriented is sufficient to produce an entire series of phenomena, of ways of living, which resemble each other. This, I think, explains the points of coincidence and discrepancy between that period on the one hand and the eleventh century and our own age on the other. Take note of it.

And now let me go back to that growing season of mankind which is the first century before and after Jesus Christ.

The situation in which man despairs of the entire sweep of his life is one of a class that we will call "extreme" situations; in these situations man finds himself facing not a whole series of ways out, but a dead end. As Spaniards say, he is between the sword and the wall.

When man feels the valueless and negative character of his existence, he first reacts against his situation, or tries to resolve it, by retiring into one corner of it in which he attempts to make himself secure—that is to say, he tries to make sure of that corner. You will realize immediately that this is a false solution, because, whether he admits it or not, he starts from a state of complete desperation. When we see him secure one corner, or one point of the vital area, we must suspect that he is not completely sincere, but that he has tried this solution in order to see what will happen, as one despairing and exasperated. I have already told you that the first stage of desperation is exasperation—that is, man denies his whole life except for a single point which, thus isolated, becomes exaggerated, exacerbated, exasperated. He pretends that life consists only of this, that this single point alone is important and the rest is nothing. Watch this, for it will clarify many things for us.

But it is undeniable that for the moment this retirement to a single point frees him from all the rest of his life, most of it vain, and simplifies it for him. The Cynic, the Christian, the Therapeutic, the Stoic, the supporter of Caesar, all plead for simplification, like the Brothers of the Common Life, or *devotio moderna*, in 1400, like Thomas à Kempis, Cusanus, Erasmus, like the Catholic monarchs who were confronting the chaos of semifeudal multiplicity—yes, now we see why!—like Luther, Montaigne, Galileo; and finally, like the genius of simplification, the man who was simplification itself, Descartes, who did not rest content with asking for simplicity but gave it, achieved it, and thereby ended the process of retirement and installed men in a simple new world, clear and firm, its very firmness made out of simplicity and clarity. His method can be reduced to this: the simple idea is the clear one, the distinct one; and vice versa, that which is clear and distinct and sure is that which is simple.

Man who is lost in complications aspires to save himself in simplicity—a universal return to nudity, a general call to rid oneself of, to retire from, to deny, all richness, complexity, and abundance. The present and the immediate past appear as bowed down with the excessive growths of their possibilities. One can think too many thoughts, want too many things, follow too many different types of life. Life is perplexity; the more possibilities there are in it, the more perplexed, the more painfully perplexed, is man. No, no; in the small courtyard of the humble Oriental dwelling, almost Andalusian in pattern, you can hear the voice of Jesus, as clear as spring water, saying "In truth, in truth, I say unto you that only one thing is necessary." Jesus is, for the moment, an extreme simplifier. St. Paul shows the logical consequences of this desire for simplicity: The law is an indomitable entangler, man loses himself in the law—away with the law! The new alliance is the only thing needed: faith—faith is enough. And note that in saying this I am not making a Lutheran out of St. Paul. When he says that faith alone saves, it is clear that what he is implying is that the law and the works which conform to the old law do not save. But he does not exclude the necessity of works in order to be saved, that is, works which issue from faith, not from the law—works which fall from the believing man as fruits from the tree which has been well nurtured in the garden.

I could go on talking for a long time about simplification as a means by which man saves himself in the crisis brought on by culture, that is to say, in the crisis produced by abundance. But I must renounce that; I, too, must rid myself of things, must simplify. I add only these three brief notes.

(1) When our present life—that is, the life of the first or the fifteenth century, modern culture, and that immediately preceding it—appeared as hatefully complicated, the desire for simplicity pushed man automatically into dreaming of the life of the past, archaic, early, and primitive: the life which existed before these complications arose. Hence a desire to return to the pristine, hence a nostalgia for the primitive life as a "return to"; and hence a turning away from complicated culture to simple culture, and even from all culture to what came before, to naked nature. We will see that this impulse toward the past is one of the impulses of the Renaissance. But no one saw this, and therefore no one understood what, from the historic point of view, the return to antiquity meant. One of the mottoes of the Renaissance which, if it showed anything, showed a movement toward the future, was this—*Philosophia duce, regredimur.*

(2) Simplification is undoubtedly the most positive thing which desperation, or its cousin, disorientation, engenders. From 1400 to 1600 there occurred a substantial simplification of life; this it has also begun today. He who now goes through the streets without a hat does not suspect, even remotely, that that vulgar act, so trivial, so material, is a way of complying docilely with the law of the times—to do without, to dispense with. And going to the opposite extreme, when, in my book *The Mission of the University*, I considered the simplification of science as unavoidable if it were to be saved, I was doing on a more serious level the same thing as does the man who goes hatless in the street.

(3) Do not forget that the desire for simplification springs forth as a reaction to excessive complication. All "reaction to" is very easily converted into "reaction

against," a reaction which is moved by such ugly passions as envy, hatred, resentment. Diogenes, the Cynic, before entering into the elegant mansion of Aristipo, his school companion under Socrates, conscientiously soiled his shoes in mud in order then to tramp it into Aristipo's rugs. This was not a matter of substituting the simplicity of mud for the complexity of rugs, but of destroying the rugs out of hatred for them.

And now, putting aside simplification in general, let us analyze one of its most curious manifestations.

Formerly, man lived as one accepting with a certain satisfaction the entire course of his life. That life was obviously composed of many dimensions, affairs, things which had to be taken account of. A culture is merely the harmonizing formula which makes it possible to face up to all, or nearly all, of these. Because they are inexorable realities, the dimensions of life and the matters which life sets before us will not allow us to ignore them. A life solution is genuine and stable only where it integrates all of these matters. In effect, culture is a work of integration, and will accept loyally all the realities that make up our existence.

But then man despairs of that culture and feels nauseated at having to integrate a life which seems to him pure nothingness. Yet as he must live on something, a very strange phenomenon is produced within him. The more central, the more serious, and the more representative of the integration which was his previous life a thing is, the more loathing, the more hatred will he feel toward it, and the more empty will it seem to him. This loathing, this hatred, will decrease in proportion as the matter is less central, more peripheral, and therefore less demanding of attention in that formula of integration. Denying all the rest, man will cling to one of these peripheral matters, to one little corner of reality, and will decide to make his entire life out of it and it alone. He will declare that this alone is important, that all the rest is contemptible. That is to say, denying all the rest, man goes from the center of life to one of its extremes.

The impulse of integration which is culture is followed by an impulse of exclusion. Here is the formal and inevitable sense in which desperation becomes extremism. Extremism is that way of life in which one tries to live only on one extreme of the vital area, with a subject, in a dimension, or with a theme which is purely peripheral. One devotes oneself to feverish affirmation of one's corner, and denies oneself the rest.

Let us clarify this with an example from our own time. Among the inexorable questions of human existence is that of social justice. It is one, undoubtedly; but also undoubtedly, it is *only* one. There are many other questions, a great many of them. Modern culture, as it could do no less, has paid some attention to social justice; but one may question whether or not it has rendered the attention which was due. Let us assume not. This would mean that in the present hierarchy of attention, social justice would rate a less peripheral place than it has, and that it would be wise to make this correction in perspective. But suppose that some despairing men resolve that there is no question other than this, or that this at least is the decisive question, the most important one, the only necessary thing, the only one which ought to occupy us; and that all the rest ought to be subordinated to it, adjusted to it, and if not adjusted and subordinated, the rest should be denied. However indisputable any single subject is, it seems essential to say that it cannot possibly rank as the central business of life. Moreover, it is probable that up to now man has not applied himself to social justice with the utmost possible care because, with the best will in the world, man cannot do very much about organizing or achieving it, just as he cannot do much about solving problems which are even more important: those of organic life, the biological problems, the problem of sorrow and death, or the terrible cosmic injustice of bodily and psychic inequalities among human beings.

The man, then, who retreats to that single question of social justice exaggerates it, becomes exacerbated and exasperated by it, removes it from its proper place, refuses with any genuineness to accept life as it is; and, by means of a personal and intimate fiction which his desperation inspires in him, he reduces life to an extreme in which he installs himself and gives himself over to extremism. And from that extreme he will fight all the rest of the enormous sector of human affairs, will deny science, morality, status, truth, and so on. Now, then; it seems a matter of argument as to whether this or any other extreme position could be adopted with any real genuineness—just as it is disputable that anyone could seriously believe that two and two make five. We are not obliged to believe him, although he swears and doubly swears to us that he is sincere, even although he lets himself be killed for it. Man frequently lets himself be killed in order to uphold his own fictions. Man has a capacity for making histrionic gestures which at times become a form of heroism. More than that, there sometimes reigns a platitudinous heroism which is not merely verbal but active, and which then becomes the peculiar form of histrionic attitude dominant in that era.

Periods of desperation open a wide field for all personal fictions and for that great histrionic power which so often shows itself in history. As men lose confidence in and enthusiasm for their culture, they are, so to speak, left hanging in midair and incapable of opposing anyone who affirms anything, who makes himself solid and secure in anything—whether it be true or be said in jest. Hence there are periods in which it is enough only to give a shout, no matter how arbitrary its phrasing, for everyone to surrender themselves to it. These are periods of *chantage* in history.

Another example: among the realities of our life, one which we glimpse but do not see clearly, is undoubtedly that of race. I say of it what I said before—at best it is a reality, but in no case is it the whole of reality, nor is it even the most basic reality. Consequently, for some thousands of years men have not paid much attention to it. Nevertheless, in periods of crisis, of exasperation, all the problems of collective life can be reduced to the matter of race—and in its name the most noble of men can be turned out of university posts. The more extreme and absurd an extremist attitude may be, the more chance it has of being imposed in the most casual fashion. Remember that St. Paul deliberately gave his faith a look of the absurd and the mad in order to make it more attractive to the exasperated folk of his period. In 1450, no less distinguished a figure than Cardinal Cusanus himself proclaimed that man's reasonable truth is constitutionally that which is not true; and that on the other hand, God's truth, the absolute truth, is characterized by the absurd. As a matter of fact, the *credo quia absurdum* always echoes in the visceral depth of Christianity.

As you see, the situation becomes extreme when man finds no solution in the normal point of view; this condition forces him to hunt an escape in a distant and eccentric extreme which formerly had seemed to him less worthy of attention. It does not matter what this is: its selection is purely arbitrary. It is not chosen for *what it is*, but mechanically and because *it is not* the customary or the consecrated, or, as we would say, the "bourgeois." Extremism is like taking a trick with a pair of deuces. One man will go to extremes with the idea of social jus-

tice and another with the idea of race; while a third or a
fourth may ally himself with something else about which
he may be arbitrary and more or less unreasonable. Un-
reasonableness is essential to extremism. To wish to be
reasonable is to renounce extremism.

You all know from the Epistles of St. Paul that in the
first Christian assemblies the believers came together to
see the truth; but they thought that they would find this
truth in the extrarational. Some of those who attended,
falling into frenzy and paroxysms, began to utter words
which had no meaning, and which others then undertook
to interpret. This frenzy was called the gift of speaking
tongues; and that very fit of dementia was considered divine inspiration. This is no place to recount how St. Paul,
who, if he did not initiate this type of frenzy, certainly
used it and greatly favored it, then strove hard to do away
with it.

Similarly, I noted several years ago that man had lost
his faith in art and that the two last generations took the
exasperated attitude of making art out of what art had
always discarded as useless—namely, material from the
fringes of human life, the area in which it touches edges
with pure imbecility—that is, with dreams, with plays on
words, with the repetition of words, with dementia, with
sexual inversions, with the puerile, with arbitrariness as
such. I classified this as *l'art de raccomander les restes*,
the art of coming to terms with what is left over, with the
residual, the detritus.

The man who despairs of culture turns against it and
declares its laws and its norms to be worn out and abolished. The mass man who in these days takes on the di-
recting of life feels himself deeply flattered by this declaration, because culture which is, after all, an authentic
imperative, weighs on him too heavily; and in that aboli-
tion of culture he sees a permit to kick up his heels, get

out of himself, and give himself over to a life of licentiousness.

Eduard Meyer, the great historian, in his book on the origins and beginnings of Christianity, *Ursprung und Anfänge des Christentums,* speaking of Simon Magus and his religious movement, says, "The campaign of St. Paul against the law led many of the sects to break out immediately into the grossest licentiousness and into complete moral disorder. In Simon's movement this naturally occurred in the highest degree."

The extreme situation, which fills man with confusion, which throws him off balance and disorients him, leads with equal ease to the best or the worst; and at first man cannot distinguish one from the other. This is natural: life is in its very self equivocal, and these are periods which lack the genuine and authentic. Remember that the origin of crisis is man's having become lost for the very reason that he loses contact with himself. Thus in periods of this sort a type of human fauna swarms which is largely equivocal, abounding in fakers and actors, which is the sadder, in that one cannot be certain as to whether any man is or is not sincere. These are turbulent times. In the fifteenth century such men as Agrippa, Paracelsus, and Savonarola moved about. What were those men? Humbugs? Sly rogues? Or authentic sages and heroes?

The probability is that they were all of these things, and not by chance or out of some peculiar personal defect. The fact is that the structure of disoriented life does not permit of firm and stable positions from which man can once and for all come to terms with himself. As I said before, man then stands on a watershed between two worlds, two forms of life, between which the individual comes and goes. Hence the contradictions in those who are properly of the Renaissance: today they are pagans, naturalists; tomorrow they will be Christians again. Nothing in that period is more frequent than biographies split between a first worldly period in which the subject is a complete libertine, and a second period of asceticism in which he renounces the ways of the first part of his life. Thus Botticelli; and thus the man who to my taste better represents the period, the enchanting Pico della Mirandola; both of them start life in a crescendo of worldly pleasure and both end—Pico still young—in sadness and desolation. Life is in a state of unstable equilibrium: humans can only mark time. Even Ficino, one of the soundest and most earnest of Renaissance men, cannot resist the pains of illness. He makes a vow to the Virgin, he recovers, and in his recovery recognizes a divine sign which makes him see that philosophy is not enough to save a soul. He throws his commentary on Lucretius into the fire and decides to dedicate all his efforts to the service of religion.

This was in the middle of the fifteenth century. But earlier the heroic pioneers of humanism acted in a fashion which was not dissimilar. Coluccio Salutati, born in 1331, boasted of Stoicism, that is, of irreligion; but his wife died and he returned to the faith. Then his sorrow faded, and he went back to framing Stoic phrases. The same thing happened to him with astrology. In general, a lack of shame was the dominant characteristic among humanists as such. In order not to focus solely on the most famous ones, in Renaudet's book, *Préréforme et humanisme à Paris pendant les premières guerres d'Italie*, study those who took classicism to France: Girolamo Balbi, Cornelius Vitelli, and Fausto Andrellini.

The man who cast the shadow of crisis before him, the one who first felt it as early as the first half of the fifteenth century, was Petrarch. He manifested all the symptoms which later became general. He was a despairing man given to arbitrary enthusiasms. His displays of melancholy—of *accidia*, as he called it—remind one of Chateaubriand. *Sento sempre nel mil coro un che d'insofato*. Completely aware of what he was saying, he tells us of himself in the same words that I used above to describe periods of crisis in general: "I find myself within the borders of two very different peoples, from whence I can see both the past and the future." Hence he lived an indecisive life, coming and going from one to the other —*ora guarda davanti, ora guarda addietro*.

Given this mode of life characterized by instability, extremism, controversy, the sudden and complete shifts which are called conversion will be very frequent. Conversion is man's change not from one idea to another, but from one definite point of view to its exact opposite: life suddenly seems to us turned upside down and inside out. That which yesterday we were burning at the stake we adore today. Hence the word which St. Paul, John the Baptist, and Jesus used: *metanoeite*—become converted, repent; that is to say, deny what you were up to this very moment and affirm your truth, recognize that you are lost. Out of this negation comes the new man who is to be constructed. St. Paul used the term again and again—*oikodume*—construction, building up from the ruins of man; out of his ashes there must be raised a new edifice. But first he must abandon the false positions he occupied and come to himself, return to his own intimate truth, which is the only firm base: this is conversion. In it the man who is lost from himself encounters the self that he has found, the self with which he is in agreement, the self which is completely one with his own truth. *Metanoia*, or conversion and repentance, is therefore none other than what I call *ensimismamiento*—withdrawal into one's self, return to oneself.

It is this *metanoia*—to become converted, or, as I prefer to say, to go back to yourself, withdraw within yourself, seek your true self—that I would urge on men today, particularly on the young. (There are too many probabilities that the generation now reading me may let themselves be led violently astray, as were the earlier generations of this and other countries, by the empty wind of some form of extremism, that is to say, by something which is substantially false. Those generations, and I fear the present generation, too, asked to be deceived—they were not disposed to surrender themselves except to something false. And to tell you a secret, I may say that my own paralysis in sectors of life other than the scientific or the academic was due to the same fear. It has not been hidden from me that I could have had almost all the youth of Spain behind me, as one man; I would have had only to pronounce a single word. But that word would have been false, and I was not disposed to invite you to falsify your lives. I know, and you will know before many more years, that all the movements which are characteristic of this moment are historically false and headed for terrible failure. There was a time when the refusal of any form of extremism carried with it the inevitable assumption that one was a conservative. But now it is becoming obvious that this is not so, because people have seen that extremism may be either radical or reactionary. My own refusal of extremism was due not to the fact that I am a conservative, which I am not; but to the fact that in it I discovered a vital and substantive fraud.

So I prefer to wait until the first genuine generation presents itself. If by any chance that is your generation, you will not have to wait long!)

All extremism inevitably fails because it consists in excluding, in denying all but a single point of the entire vital reality. But the rest of it, not ceasing to be real merely because we deny it, always comes back and back, and imposes itself on us whether we like it or not. The history of all forms of extremism has about it a monotony which is truly sad; it consists in having to go on making pacts with everything which the particular form of extremism under discussion had pretended to eliminate.

This happened with Christianity. For it would be useless to try to hide with pretty phrases the fact that Christianity, both in its beginning and in its strictest forms, is a kind of extremism. More than that, one can understand its genesis only when one has understood the life plan of extremism. This is one reason why I have spent so much time on its analysis. Christianity, too, consisted in pointing out and isolating a particular dimension of life which ancient man had more or less ceased to heed. But if we note which dimension that was, we find that it has characteristics which are peculiar and in some ways unique; these remove it from the realm of competition and explain why this Christian extremism alone managed to take root—I do not say managed to win, because to win, to triumph in the truest sense, is not possible for any form of extremism except in the degree to which it ceases to be extremism, as in this case.

In the very beginning, Christianity started by being different from all the other creeds of its time which were born out of desperation in that it was more radical, more basic, than the others; and it was the only one which was consistent with its desperation. Let me explain what I mean.

What is the prospect in view of which man customarily lives? A while ago, you found, as one finds every day, that you had inexorably to do something, to make something, because that is what living is. Various possibilities of doing opened to you, which therefore were possibilities of being, of living, at some future moment. You could go to this place or that, or could not go anywhere, but had to stay where you were. To stay is as much a matter of doing as is its opposite. Out of these possibilities you chose one: to read this book, to dedicate or to fill a piece of your life, for which there is no substitute, by becoming my readers. But this you decided for a specific reason and for some purpose. More than once I have told you that I could name the different types of motives in view of which, on account of which, you made your choice. Perhaps you would be surprised that I know part of your secrets, secrets which you have told to no one. Some day I may give a lecture to be entitled "Why Are You There?" But there is no time now. Whatever the motives that moved you, they will always include the fact that you decided to do this thing at this moment—to come here, to be my readers—for the reason that you are thinking of doing something else and being somewhere else tomorrow, and you think of that because day after tomorrow or another day later on, you will think of being and doing something else; and so in order to decide what you were going to do this afternoon you planned the entire line of your life as it now parades itself before you. You decided on this act of reading my pages because it had meaning as a link in the chain of your entire life.

Whether you like it or not, the fact of deciding on one specific act implies man's justifying it at the bar of his own spirit. That justification consists in seeing that this act is a good way to achieve another which appears as its end; but this other, in turn, is the way toward another, and so on up to the very last that we are able to anticipate. This is the perspective within which we are accustomed to live: each of our actions remains justified by the series of actions which we assume are going to make up our entire life. We are constantly seeking an internal justification for life.

But more than once we have surprised ourselves thinking as follows: I do this, that, or the other in order to live; but this living of mine, taking it as a whole, from birth to death—has it any meaning? The relative justification which the various acts of my life have in relation to one another has no value if the total act of living cannot be justified. It would be necessary for some one of the things we do in living to have an absolute value. Well, now; there is nothing in the interior of our lives which seems completely satisfactory and which is justified in and by itself. In itself our experience is a strange reality, empty of sense, which consists in being something which by definition is nothing, is the being of nothing, is the pretense of something positive which remains pure frustrated pretense. If the sum and entirety of living lacks meaning, if one lives for nothing, then all the internal justifications which I find for my life in its acts are an error of perspective. This conclusion imposes a radical change, another perspective.

It is obvious that this new perspective can be adopted only by one who has ceased to be interested in the internal web of life, who, ideally, has separated himself from vital matters and who looks at crowds and swarmings from afar and with the eye of a bird; in short, one who has moved so far toward the furthest extreme of existence as to have emerged resolutely from that existence. All of us have at one time or another come to the point of asking ourselves this question and adopting this point of view. To think thus, to wonder if life really has any meaning or not, is one of the many things which we are able to do and which, in fact, we have all done at some time. But we have not definitely installed ourselves within this thought, we have not lived on or out of this thought. On the contrary: life courted us with its pleasures, its attractions, with all sorts of incitements; and we preferred to occupy ourselves with its apparent internal richness, to make use of another perspective which we might call the intravital, to live exclusively on that preoccupation with the total value of life.

We can do this because we are not truly and completely despairing. The things of life still distract and amuse us. But he who despairs of intravital matters, of all that holds the web of life together, must, if he is to be consistent within himself, always place himself in that dimension which consists of perceiving the lack of meaning which life has as a whole. He will, then, be a typical extremist. Out of what is only one thought among many he will make his only thought, his obsession, if you will. It will be seen that unlike the others, this form of extremism does not arbitrarily stand firm on one point of life; on the contrary, it affirms the negation of the whole of life. And, *ipso facto,* this negation is converted into something which is most positive. The despairing man realizes that this—the act of despairing—is not something which may or may not happen to him, something from which, if it should happen, he could free himself; but that it is his very being, his nature. This life in its very substance is naught else but desperation. Man is a reality which cannot value itself: he is not in his own hands, he does not sustain or uphold himself. To despair is to feel that we are constitutionally impotent, that we depend entirely on something outside and distinct from ourselves.

The perspective within which we are accustomed to move makes us believe that man with nature about him is enough so that his life may be somewhat positive. This is the fundamental error of which he must be cured, and the very definition of sin which St. Augustine gives in his *De civitate dei: "sibi quodam modo fieri atque esse principium"*—to believe that one is the source of one's being and doing; in short, to create for oneself illusions about oneself. For the Christian, the essential sinner is the man who has confidence in himself, who still expects something of himself.

On the other hand, man finds his own truth when he recognizes that he cannot, with any meaning, live out of himself alone, when he discovers his basic dependence—and placing himself wholly in the hands of the superior power, of God, prepares himself to live on and from Him. For example, man attempts to discover truth through his reason. Vain attempt! Truth is found only when man declares himself incapable of it, and is prepared not to search for it, but to receive it through revelation. Into revelation man puts nothing more than his good desire—God supplies the rest. And so it is in everything else: when man recognizes that he is nothing, he makes of himself an emptiness which God fills to the brim. It is the same thing that always happens when we recognize an error. Previously, while we were still in the midst of the error, we thought we had something positive; we now see that it was an error, therefore something negative; and this discovery, being pure truth, is what is truly positive.

In this fashion the Christian, by a line of argument which is automatic, converts desperation into salvation. The new perspective makes him see the true reality of this life, which consists in not being this life—coming, going, counting on this or that, knowing this or that bit of partial and relative knowledge—this life is not the true reality, but merely an optical error. It is only a moment of refraction in the time-span of our eternal life. And one must behave accordingly; that is, in place of justifying our intravital acts one with another, we are to submit ourselves to our absolute life in God—in short, to live each moment over and above this life and its surrounding nature, to translive, as in eternity. Man, as a natural being confronting the natural world, has died; and only the supernatural dimension, the absolute meaning of his acts, will interest him. Thus man remains alone with God. He ceases to depend on the world, which is only a barrier to the relations of the soul with God; and if he does look at it, he will see it only as a pure reflection of the divine, as a symbol and an allegory. Such a man will scorn science. For two reasons: because science takes the world more seriously than the world merits; and because it assumes the confidence of man in his natural reason, which is at the very least a tendency to sin, to living centered in oneself. The life of a Christian is theocentric, centered in God; and the world to him is the supernatural other world.

But it is here that this extremist, like every other one, is going to have to compromise. That denial of the intra-worldly is an arbitrary exclusion. Man, on coming to an understanding with God, travels dully through the world and is incapable of understanding it. God, apparently, does not reveal the laws of nature. Nature begins to reclaim the rights which it possessed as a reality, and little by little will begin again to interpose itself between man and God. The Catholic Gilson, in his book *L'esprit de la philosophie médiévale*, sees this and says it very well: "At the end of the thirteenth century the world of science—that is, purely human science—begins to interpose itself between us and the divine and symbolic universe of the late Middle Ages." The Renaissance crisis is coming into being. Nature is again going to be separating man from God. And when Galileo and Descartes discover a new type of science, of human reason, which makes it possible to predict cosmic events with a high degree of exactitude, man recovers his confidence and his faith in himself. He goes back to living on and from himself, more than ever before in history. That was the modern age—humanism.

10

Milestones in Christian Thought

If, in the two previous chapters, I have managed to satisfy certain very justifiable curiosities which I am assuming in you, I must now go back to the demands of my theme, and as briefly as possible catch up with the time, which I do not believe lost, but which we have certainly been spending.

Let us return to our fundamental idea. Our life, human life, is for every one of us the basic fundamental reality. It is the only thing which we have and which we are. Well, then; life consists in the fact that man, not knowing how it came about, finds himself having to exist within surroundings which are settled and inexorable. One lives here and now, without choice or remedy. The environment within which we must live and sustain ourselves includes our material surroundings, and also our social surroundings, the society in which we find ourselves. As this environment as such is something other than man, something different, something strange, something alien to him, the fact of existing within these surroundings cannot mean that man lies passively inert in them and forms part of them. Man does not form a part of his environment; on the contrary, he always finds himself in an attitude of facing up to it. The act of living is the having to do something so that our surroundings shall not annihilate us. This living, then, constitutes a problem, a question, a difficulty to be resolved.

Our life is given to us—we did not give it to ourselves —but it is not given to us ready-made. It is not a thing whose being is fixed once and forever, but a task, something which has to be created—in short, a drama. Thus it is that man must very speedily create ideas about his circumstances, must be able to interpret them, in order to be able to decide on all the other things which he has to do. Hence the first response which man makes on becoming aware that he is living, that is to say, submerged in his environment, is to believe something about it. Man is always in the grip of a belief, and in the midst of things he lives out of that belief, in conformity with it.

The modern era, whose genesis we are now studying, made a terrible blunder by clinging to the belief that man's primary being consists in thinking, that his basic relationship with things is an intellectual relationship. This error is called "idealism." The crisis which we are suffering is none other than the price we must pay for that error. Thought is not man's being; man does not consist of thought; thought is only an instrument, a faculty which he possesses neither more nor less than he possesses a body. His being, let us repeat, is a great occupation, and not a thing already given to him, as are his body and his mental mechanism. Nevertheless, thinking is the first thing which man does as a reaction to the basic dimension of his life, which is the having to come to terms with his environment.

Granted, as we said before, that this environment is not limited to the material things about us, but also includes the human society into which we have fallen; the result is that each man finds, as forming part of his surroundings, the system of beliefs, the concept or interpretation of the world, which is operative in that society at that time. Whether he allows himself to become part of it, or to combat it and oppose to it something else which originates within himself, man has no recourse but to take account of the beliefs of his time; and it is this dimension of his environment which makes of man an entity which is in essence historic. Or, to put it another way, man is never original man, the first to arrive on the scene, but always a successor, an inheritor, a son of the human past. He must always live at a moment which is fixed by a process previous to his being; he sees himself obliged to make his entrance on stage at one precise instant in the very broad human drama which we call "history."

Out of that drama we are taking only the brief section with which this book is concerned; here is a very rapid description of the scenes that make it up.

Scene One. Finding himself in a desperate situation, or in an environment of which he despairs, man makes himself a Christian; that is, he reacts with the Christian interpretation of life.

Man hefts the entire mass of his life possibilities, asks himself how much he is worth as a natural being, and finds that he cannot value himself, that this life is powerless to resolve itself, and hence that natural man and his existence cannot be the true reality. How can a thing be real which is not sufficient unto itself either for the purpose of giving itself being or of achieving success in that being? How can human life be in truth a thing which is sufficient if no one can be sure that he can complete the phrase, "My life is . . . something." Life is continually in the immediate danger of being destroyed. What reality it has is only such as is necessary to make us realize that its effective reality is not within it, but outside it. Man is not a sufficient, an adequate, being, but on the contrary an indigent, a needy being, needing someone else on whom to lean. Or to put it another way, this life is only the mask of another more real life which sets it up, completes it, explains it, and justifies it.

In this way the desperate man, recognizing the nothingness, the insufficiency, of his life in itself, discovers the

need for admitting another existence and another solid
reality. But that other life is discovered dialectically, as
an exact counterpoise to the one we have and the one we
lead. That other reality appears with attributes which are
completely opposed to the natural human reality: it has
neither beginning nor end, it is timeless and eternal, it is
its own beginning, it is omnipotent, and so on. In short,
that reality is God.

Having made this discovery, and starting from this belief, we will live our lives according to a new perspective.
Everything that life is, everything we do in it, we will
refer to our true reality, that is, to what we are before
God or in God. Thus we absorb our temporal existence
back into God's eternity. Man prepares to live with his
back to this life and his face turned to the life beyond.

Note well the radical transformation of the world, of
all that is ordinarily considered to be reality, which this
shift represents. In older days, the Greek man, whom
Christianity will now call the pagan, thought reality
meant the aggregate of those psycho-corporeal things
which make up the cosmos: the stone, the plant, the animal, the man, the star; that is, all that can be seen and
touched, plus what can be assumed as the invisible and
intangible ingredient of what can be seen and touched.
When the Greek meditated on this reality and tried to
discover its essential structure, he arrived at such concepts
as substance, cause, quality, movement, and so on; in
short, the categories of the cosmic being. But to Christianity, reality signifies something which is not corporeal
or even psychic; to the Christian true reality lies in
man's behavior with God—in something so immaterial,
so incorporeal, that to call it spiritual, as was common, is
to give it too much of a material character.

Using our terminology, the Christian world is composed solely of God and man, face to face, linked in a re-

lationship which might be called purely moral, if one did not better call it ultramoral. None of the cosmic categories of the Greek serve to interpret and describe that strange reality which consists not in being this or that, in the manner of the stone, the plant, the animal, and the star, but in being as a course of conduct. What this Christian reality assumes is that man feels himself absolutely dependent on another superior Being; or, what is the same thing, that he sees himself essentially as an infant. And so that he may exist as a child, living must mean not the power of independent existence on his own account, but on God's account and in constant reference to Him. Thus for the pure Christian the world, that is, this world, and nature lack interest. Worse yet, attention to nature easily leads man to believe that it is something permanent and sufficient, leads him to fall into the intraworld point of view, in a desire to live for it and from it. Hence the disdain which the first-century Christians had for all worldly occupations, for politics, economics, and science. The only things that were truly real to them were the soul and God. Soul is the traditional word by which one designates the I. St. Augustine, prototype of the man made Christian, of the converted, will say: *Deum et animam scire cupio. Nihilne plus? Nihil omnino.*

This position is perfectly logical in a Christian extremist, that is to say, in a man who wishes to be only a Christian. Well, then; if for him there is no reality properly described as such except the *Deus exuperantissimus* and the relation of the child with Him, it is evident that the concepts of Greek philosophy derived from the process of analyzing the pseudo reality of the cosmos serve for nothing. And here you have the reason why, in a previous chapter, I dared to say that what has been called Christian philosophy was rather a kind of intellectual betrayal of Christianity's genuine intuition. St. Augustine, being a genius, tried to discover new concepts adequate to the new reality; and it can be said without excessive error that whatever there is of actual Christian philosophy is due to him.

But no one man, however much of a genius, was enough; it was necessary to un-think all the old concepts, to free oneself from them, and to forge an ideology which should be original from the roots up. The enormous and very subtle mass of Greek ideology weighing heavily on those germinal hours of Christian thought crushed it. And one can be even more precise; it is possible that if there had been no Plato among the Greeks, the Christian of those first centuries might have achieved the full scope of his inspiration, might have immunized himself against the arch-worldly ideology of those Hellenes who thought with their eyes and their hands. But Plato was an irresistible seducer; there was in him an extrinsic likeness to the Christian trend. He, too, talked of two worlds—this world and the other world—and echoed rumors of a life beyond this earth. St. Augustine himself recognized in Platonism the best introduction to the Christian faith. But, although I cannot now take time to prove it, one must admit that in this there was something of a *quid pro quo*. Platonism is in no sense Christianity.

One cannot reach the absolute reality which God is to the Christian as one can reach the other world of Platonic ideas, by means of reason which is a faculty, a gift of the natural man, something he has, possesses, and manages on his own account. Platonic ideas had only to be what they were for man to be able more or less to understand them. But the existence of the Christian God is of such transcendent nature that there is no road which leads from man to it. In order that this be understood, God, in addition to being what He is, must also take care to discover Himself to man—in short, reveal Himself. The most characteristic attribute of the Christian God is this: *Deus ut revelans*. Compared with the entire Greek system of ideas, the idea of revelation, like the idea of creation, is an absolute novelty. Note well the paradox involved. In the concept of revelation it is not the subject, man, who by his own activity knows the object, God, but the opposite—it is the object, God, who gives Himself to be known, who causes the subject to know Him. This strange fashion of knowledge, in which man does not go to seek the truth and take possession of it, but, on the contrary, truth comes to seek the man and take possession of him, inundate him, penetrate him—this is faith, divine faith.

Moreover, for the pure Christian with the burning soul of an African who was St. Augustine, there was no other knowledge than that. There is—and mark this well, because it is the specific characteristic of the first scene which we are describing—there is no human reason. What we customarily call human reason is the use we make of the constant illumination with which God favors us. Man by himself alone is not capable of thinking the simple truth that two and two make four. The intuition of all truth, what we call *sensu stricto*, "intellectual," is the operation of God in us.

To such a degree was this true that in those first years life for the Christian consisted exclusively in accommodating himself to God. Hence every occupation involving the things of the world lost meaning and came to be valued only as a sad compromise with human weakness. Properly speaking, man lived only when he occupied himself with God, in intellectual and loving contemplation, or in acts of charity which were begun and executed only as gestures toward God. This meant that the pure Christian had to be a priest or a monk or something similar. All other human offices, all other occupations, were, in principle, ways of going astray. Work in which man involves himself with the things of this world is not man's substantive destiny, but a penalty or a punishment which man has borne since his expulsion from Paradise; or else it is a mortification of the flesh which he imposes upon himself voluntarily in order to enter into sainthood; or a supplementary and ornamental effort begun as a form of worshipping God.

Scene Two: St. Augustine lived between the fourth and fifth centuries. If we now leap six centuries ahead we find the structure of Christian life somewhat modified. The Augustinian motto was *Credo ut intelligam*—in order to know it is first necessary to believe; therefore, strictly speaking, there is no knowledge as a thing apart and for itself. To know is, at root, to receive revelations and illuminations—consequently, to believe. God is the only thing which truly is. Man, considered by himself, has no reality.

But is this not excessive? When an illumination is born in man, however passive his role is thought to be, he does something in order to receive it. God is generous: man is poor and a beggar. Out of his richness God gives something to man, puts that something in man's hand as He might put an ounce of gold. But the beggar has necessarily, and at the very least, to close his hand over the given ounce—otherwise the good will which God shows in making such a gift would be lost. Thus in the field of knowledge God breathes into us a truth by means of faith; He puts faith into us. But this faith which comes from God to us must be assimilated, that is to say, it must be understood. The content of faith is the word of God which comes to man; but man must understand that word. It does not matter whether that word announces a mystery or not. Even an inexplicable mystery must, in order to be a mystery, be understood as such. I do not

explain the squared circle to myself; but I do not explain
it for the very reason that I understand what those words
signify.

However firm the Augustinian thesis desires to be in
the matter of every truth coming to us from God, there
will be a point in the process of reception at which it is
no longer God who breathes truth into us, but man who
makes it his, who, working with his natural gifts, thinks
it. In his extremist fervor, St. Augustine was occupied
solely with the origin of truth, in the last analysis divine;
and he paid no attention to that stage of knowledge in
which man does not limit himself to believing on God's
account, but inevitably reflects, understands, and reasons
on his own account. To overlook this, to be preoccupied
solely with God, was basically the structure of Christian
life in the first scene of the drama. But by the tenth century generations and generations had been born already
installed in the Christian life, and for them this was not
so dramatically the question as it was for St. Augustine.
Thus their attention had room to occupy itself with the
second stage of the process, the arguable intervention of
man in the reception of the Divine word. No: man may
be very little, but he is not simply nothing. In order that
there may be faith, he must intervene, whether he wants
to or not, inasmuch as he needs to understand faith, which
is the word of God.

Such is the situation of St. Anselmo. We are now in the
eleventh century. Compared with the motto of St. Augustine, *Credo ut intelligam,* that of St. Anselmo is *Fides
quaerens intellectum.* Formerly intelligence, lost and feeling itself nothing, needed faith. Now it is faith, which,
in order to complete itself, has need of intelligence. This
does not mean that man, once God has revealed Himself through faith, will try to reconstruct the whole content of faith by means of pure human reasoning, after

which he might dispense with faith. No: what this means is that the intellect must work on faith and within faith in order to provide it with its peculiar illumination—in a way, the intellect must do what acid does when it works on an etched plate.

An example will make this clearer to you, for fast as I am going, and forced to trace only straight and deliberately simple lines, I do wish to be understood. Let me say then, as a clarifying comparison, that our vision shows us or puts before us the natural phenomenon of colors. Without this bit of information, brought us by the visual sense, it would never occur to us to think of light and its chromatic quality. Well, now; that sensory notice is a crude and irrational fact which we encounter, which moves us to exercise our intellect on it in order to make light and its colors intelligible to us. This intellectual task, a rational acting on the irrational data given by vision, is called optics. The operation of intelligence on the content of faith is somewhat similar. For the very reason that St. Anselmo believed on bended knee that the absolute reality is God, His Trinity, His omnipotence, and so on, he saw himself obliged to understand as a natural man all that of which he was notified supernaturally.

This signifies a very important change in the structure of Christian life; thanks to this, man, who earlier found himself made nothing, now begins his own affirmation, assumes his confidence in his own natural gifts. If, on the one hand, he needs the supernatural illumination of faith, on the other, the result is that this in turn needs illumination from man. Human reason begins to take shape within faith. Revelation, the word of God, must be integrated with a human science of the divine word. This science is scholastic theology. For generation after generation, from St. Anselmo on, the role of reason goes on growing within faith, and Christian extremism begins to covenant with man and with nature, which it started out by excluding.

Scene Three: Two centuries later. Noon of the Middle Ages. St. Thomas. The Christian recognizes in the purely human reason represented by the Greeks, especially Aristotle, a substantive power which stands apart from faith and is independent of it. Now it is no longer a matter of the intelligence lit by God reworking the Divine word in order to clarify it, as it was with St. Anselmo. Now the intelligence is a separate field, and fundamentally different from faith. St. Thomas fixes the borders between the one and the other with exactness. There is blind faith and there is evident reason. The latter lives by itself and with its own roots and beginnings, face to face with the other. Always within the absolute reality, which is God, there is marked off a space within which the child, the man, acts on his own account. In other words, an ordinance for man is recognized and he regains consciousness of his power and his rights; moreover, he now has an obligation to affirm his natural qualities, and, above all his reason. Considered in relation to the whole Christian past, St. Thomas reduces the exclusive territory of faith to a minimum and widens to the maximum the role of human science in matters of theology. This difference in the relative sizes of both territories is compensated for by the range of truths which reach us solely through revelation. Thanks to this, one may talk of an equilibrium between faith and reason, between the supernatural and the natural. To a Christian of the first century this equilibrium, this recognition of human reason as a free power, would necessarily have seemed a horror; and he would have felt himself sniffing abominable paganism.

Today the Catholic Church finds itself installed, perhaps involved, in Thomism, within which it has lived for centuries, and which has been converted for it into an inveterate habit. For this very reason the Church does not clearly perceive what St. Thomas signified historically, and what it was that in his own period gave rise to such bitter struggles within his own breast. St. Thomas was a tremendous humanist. With superlative energy he proclaimed the rights of rationalism; and this means, and do not let it shock you, that he put something of God into many quarters within the world. Reason, the natural gift of man, has a radius of action; so far as it reaches, all that I can understand by means of reason is nature, is within my horizon, and is in this world of ours.

This being true, all the other qualities and conditions which have been ascribed to God, except for certain divine attributes, are also open to reason. In the same degree, then, He ceases to be *exuperantissimus*, and goes back to being, like the God of Aristotle, one of many ingredients in the cosmos.

St. Thomas could think this way because his rationalist enthusiasm made him think of God as the reasonable Being *par excellence*. God is, first of all, intellect and reason; in short, He *is* logic. This divine logic, intelligence, and reason are infinite, while man's logic, intelligence, and reason are limited. But this implies that both have a common texture, although in capacity the one greatly exceeds the other.

Human reason coincides with a part of the divine rational Being, which, in that part, is completely transparent to our thought, in short, is intelligible. Thus it is that man, although simply as man and without God's direct aid, can, by the mere employment of his natural gifts, deal with God.

If you now think back to the first scene of the drama, you will note that Christian life has profoundly changed in structure. It is not that God has grown smaller; but it

is undeniable that man has grown larger. He is no longer
a being despairing of himself; and when he confronts
God he has confidence in his nature, insofar as his limitations allow.

And with man reaffirmed, the world about him reap-
pears with its rights of existence brought to his attention;
Christians are no longer occupied solely with theology.
Philosophy also occupies itself with things, and cosmol-
ogy is created. Almost all the knowledge of the Greeks
about the world is relearned by Christian clerics. Faculties
of philosophy begin to move into the first rank, and to
astonish the theologians.

I note here in passing what will later become a most
important fact, that all this new faith of man in himself,
a faith which is still relative and which does not exclude
his consciousness as a child of God who has at last become independent, arises in the name of a most particular
form of reason—purely logical reason, which is based on
the evidence of the conceptual relations between kind
and species. It is the old reason of Aristotle, which becomes concrete in the syllogism. Man has no hint of any
other kind of reason. That alone is intelligible to him
which is obtained by means of syllogistic inference, and
this assumes that universal substances exist in reality. If
there were only individual men, this one, that one, the
other one, it would not be possible to forge an adequate
syllogism, which must always arise from some true affirmation about man in general. Hence nature must include man in general, a concept which was called the
universal man.

Scene Four: The high noon of Thomism, like every
midday, lasts only a short time. The morning is long, it
unrolls slowly. The afternoon is also slow moving. But
noon—by the time noon arrives it is already departing.

Two generations after St. Thomas a Scot toppled the

edifice and precipitated the Middle Ages rapidly and ir-remediably toward their crisis and consummation.

St. Thomas was born in 1225 or 1226, Duns Scotus around 1270. As it is still disputed whether certain works which were traditionally attributed to him did or did not belong to him, I am going to refer, to the writings as a whole and to their tendency rather than to Duns Scotus himself. The general characteristic of these writings is the battle against Thomism.

In Thomism European man had achieved a harmony between faith and reason, God and nature. The key to this harmony, as we have seen, was that man, in facing the reality which is God and the world, could trust in himself more than a little. God is rational; and because He is rational, so is his work—man and the world. Reason, then, is the harmonic nexus, the bridge between man and the surroundings with which he must deal.

But Scotism protested against this paganization of Christianity; it wished to return, so far as God is concerned, to pure Christian inspiration. It is false, argued Scotus, to assert that God consists primarily of reason, of intelligence; and that He conducts Himself by submitting perforce to the rational and intelligent. That is to decrease God's stature and in addition to deny His most characteristic function, that of constituting the beginning of being. All being is because God is. But God is not God for anything else, for any other reason, for any other cause, from any other motive. God is not God because it is necessary that He so be—this would mean submitting God to a necessity and imposing on Him the greatest of obligations, that of existing. No: God exists and He is what He is because He so desires, and for no other reason. Only thus can He be truly the beginning of Himself and of everything. In short, God is will, pure will, antedating everything else, including reason. God could behave irrationally; He is capable of everything, including the refusal to be. If He preferred to create reason and even to submit Himself to it, it is simply because He so wished, and therefore the existence of rationality is a fact but not a principle. In His authentic being, God is irrational and unintelligible. Therefore a theological science such as scholasticism was creating is illusory. Theology is a practical science which does not discover truths about God, but only teaches man how to handle the dogmas of faith. Therefore it remains basically dissociated from reason. Man goes back to having no means of his own with which to deal with God; on the other hand, his increased degree of reason has a large field of action in worldly things.

Scene Five: Half a century later. The doctrine of Duns Scotus obliged man to live in a double world, whose two halves had nothing to do with one another: the divine world above, before which he has no means of his own, and this world, for which he possesses the vigorous faculty which is his reason. In the face of God, man is lost, because faith is the irrational element. In exchange he has the world.

But William of Occam demonstrated that in the world universals do not exist; what we call "man," "dog," "stone," are not realities, but fictions of our own, simple and verbal titular signs of which we avail ourselves in order to move about among things which are always singular; this man, that tree. But this means no less than that the old logic of the syllogism—conceptual reason—has no value for the understanding of realities.

For medieval man this was a catastrophe. Lost in God's presence in a vague and habitual dependence on faith, he is now lost in the world of things, face to face with them, one by one, having to live with his senses, that is to say, by means of the pure experience of what he is seeing, hearing, and touching. And in fact the later Parisian followers of Occam, Oresme and Buridan, were the initiators of a new form of intellectual relationship between man and things: experimental reason. But for the moment not even this existed. Only the failure of the other doctrine, of conceptual reason or pure logic, occupied men's minds.

The irrational God who communicates bureaucratically with men by means of the ecclesiastical organization remains in the background of life's human landscape. On the other hand, the failure of logical reason is due to the acuteness of man himself, who has dissolved it by means of his own analysis. Therefore he is left with an extraordinary confidence in himself which he cannot justify. He finds himself lost; but at the same time he has a profound hope and a new illusion concerning this life. Nature interests him, above all because of its beauty. He feels an appetite for social values—power, glory, riches. Lost, but full of illusion—this is the man of the fifteenth century. The crisis begins; but it is very different, in a certain way completely opposite, from the crisis in which Christianity took root. Then man despaired of himself and for that reason went to God. Now man despairs of the Church—read the constant complaints which were being made about the Church from 1400 to 1500; he detaches himself from God; and he remains alone with things. But he has faith in himself; he has a feeling that he is going to find within himself a new instrument to resolve his struggle with his environment, a new reason, a new science, the *nuova scienza* of Galileo. Modern physics is germinating. In 1500 Copernicus was studying in Bologna. A few years earlier Leonardo had said, "*Il sole no si muove*." Nature was about to surrender to physico-mathematical reason, which is a technical reasoning. And about this time Ferdinand and Isabella create the first European state and invent the reason of state. Those two forms of reason make up modern man.

11

Fifteenth-Century Man

THE previous chapter was like a film in which we watched the essential movement of European man from the fifth century to the dawn of the fifteenth century. History, in one of its dimensions, is cinematographic. Each man lives in a present moment, in a vital landscape, in a world, in a system of beliefs—all these expressions are synonymous—which ordinarily, at least in its great topographic outlines, is quiet. But that landscape, that structure of life, changes in every generation; each one of the generations may be motionless, like each frame in a cinema film; but the process of succession imparts movement.

On the other hand, I hope that as you watched this film unroll you noticed that its changes are neither sudden, nor produced by chance; on the contrary, one form of life issues from the previous form with exemplary continuity and as though obeying a law of transformation. In short, the historic reality, the human destiny, advances dialectically, although that basic dialectic of life is not, as Hegel believed, a conceptual dialectic composed of pure reason, but the dialectic of a reason much broader, deeper, and richer than pure reason—the dialectic of life, of living reason.

But it is clear that if, on reconstructing the past by means of history, we find each new period or epoch emerging from the previous one with a certain logic—or if, in other words, each form of life is succeeded by another which comes not by chance, but exactly as predetermined in the earlier period—this means that the contrary will in some measure also be possible. That is, when living in a specific period, one can foresee the general lines of the immediate future; in short, prophecy, in all seriousness, is possible. Schlegel used to say that a historian is a prophet in reverse; and I maintain that this remark implies that the prophet is a historian in reverse—he is a man who tells the story of the future by anticipation. The matter is a very delicate one, and I am not going into it at any length; but it is so basic to my fashion of understanding not only history but also metaphysics, that I must say a dozen words about it.

It is obvious that history, the reconstruction of the past, operates under conditions which are incomparably more favorable than those surrounding prophecy, the prediction of the future. The historian has all the data in his hands, all the details of the integrating process out of which he is going to derive history from its beginning to its end. He needs only to discover the organic meaning of those data. In respect to the future, we find ourselves facing an opposite situation: of the process which is going to happen we have neither the data nor the details. This is enough to show that man's prophetic ability is much more limited and difficult to exercise than is his historic. There is no reason even to suggest that man could predict any such amount, any such span, of the future as he can narrate of the past. Today we can, with some clarity, describe four thousand years of the past. No one would pretend that we could similarly foretell four thousand years of the future.

Nevertheless, you should note that an essential characteristic of the historic perspective—as of the visual—is that it loses clarity in proportion to the increase in the distance. We see the centuries nearest us much more intimately than those which are remote; with certain peculiar exceptions we can say more about the life forms of the immediate past than about those of the more distant past; when we reach back to the eighth or ninth century before Christ, we can say only things that are very general, and if one chooses to call general things vague, we can say only very vague things. This law of perspective is greatly accentuated when it comes to predicting the future; but in principle it is identical.

In this statement, I am suggesting that the narrow limits and the genuine difficulties surrounding man's prophetic power—a power which is, after all, a matter of degree—ought not to be confused with the existence of this prophetic ability, with the question as to whether man can in the last analysis, predict anything, whether much or little.

Having stated the matter thus precisely, I am going to say the following. First, if human life is not a reality— with its being, consistency, and content given to man already made, as these are given to the stone and the star—but is such that it must be made by man himself, then every life is a constant prophecy and composed of its own substance; for whether we like it or not, life is essentially an anticipation of the future. The more genuine the conduct of our lives, the more authentic will be the prediction of the future.

The first sign of this authenticity lies in taking account of the fact that the periphery of our life, that which, as we say, "happens to us," is not in our hands, nor have we in our hands the essential matter of not dying in the next instant. But at the same time there is surely in our hands the true meaning of how much is happening to us, because that depends on what we decide to do. Moment by moment man has open before him many different possibilities of being—he may do this, or that, or the other. From this it follows that he has no remedy but to choose one of them. And obviously if he chooses one, if he now decides to do this and not the other, it is because this doing fulfills for him some part of the general project of life which he has decided for himself. Living, then, is a matter of not being able to take one step without anticipating the direction or the general meaning of all the others which will be taken throughout one's life.

Things being thus, the question concerning man's prophetic gift turns inside out. How can he fail to be able to prophesy, if, at least in respect to the general meaning of his own life, it is man himself who decides what that life and its meaning are going to be? At least in that sense and within those limits, to live is to prophesy, to anticipate the future.

That program of living which each one of us is, which gives to what happens to us its internal and positive content—remember that the same thing, when happening to different men, acquires in each of them a different meaning; thus the identical fact of reading what I write is for each one of you a vital occurrence with a profile which is more or less different—well, then; that program of life which each person is, is clearly the work of his imagination. If man did not have the psychological mechanism of imagining, man would not be man. The stone, in order to be a stone, has no need to construct in fancy what it is going to be; but man has. We all know very well that we have constructed diverse programs of life within which we oscillate, first realizing one and then another. In one of its essential dimensions, then, human life is a work of imagination. Man constructs himself, whether he wishes to or not—hence the profound phrase of St. Paul, *oikodumein*, the need that man be a builder. In principle we construct ourselves exactly as the novelist constructs his personages. We are the novelists of our selves; and if we did not irrevocably play that role in our own lives, you may be quite sure that we would not be novelists in the literary or poetic world.

But now we come to the most important thing. Those diverse projects or programs of life which our fancy elaborates, and among which our will, another psychic mechanism, can freely choose, are not presented to us as looking all alike; a strange voice emerging from some intimate and secret depth of our own calls on us to choose one of these and to bar the others. All these programs, please note, are presented to us as possible—we may have the ability to be one kind of person or another, but one and only one appears to us as the one which we have to be. This is the strangest and most mysterious ingredient in man. On the one hand, he is free, he is not forced to be any single thing, as is the star; and yet in the face of this freedom something always rises with a certain character of necessity about it, as though saying to us, "You are able to be whatever you want; but only if you choose this or that specific pattern will you be what you have to be." That is to say, among his various possible beings each man always finds one which is his genuine and authentic being. The voice which calls him to that authentic being is what we call "vocation." But the majority of men devote themselves to silencing that voice of the vocation and refusing to hear it. They manage to make a noise within themselves, to deafen themselves, to distract their own attention in order not to hear it; and they defraud themselves by substituting for their genuine selves a false course of life. On the other hand, the only man who lives his own self, who truly lives, is the man who lives his vocation, whose life is in agreement with his own true self.

Now, then; that true self of every one of us, that program of life described as following a calling, includes all fields of existence and does not refer solely to the profession or the occupation which we are going to choose. It refers, for example, to the field of thoughts or opinions. Each one of us can hold whatever opinions he wishes, but only a certain group of those possible opinions constitutes what he must think if he wishes to think according to his vocation. And if he persists in adhering to other opinions he will live in intellectual conflict with his own self.

But when I insist so strongly on the fact that each man has a life program which is the only one genuinely his own, I do not mean you to understand, and thereby misunderstand, that the opinions which a man must hold should necessarily be different from those which his neighbor must hold. On the contrary, the greater part of what we must be in order to be genuinely ourselves is common to other men in the same stage of the long human destiny; that is, to other men of our period. I may, if I wish, think that two and two are five; but an inner voice shouts at me that I am not really thinking that, that I must know that two and two are four. Very well, this is not peculiar to me; we must all think the same in whatever categories fall strictly within the circle of science.

It is the fate of modern man, whether he wants to or not, to have to think scientifically, that is, in conformity with strict reasoning in everything which falls within the orbit of science. Within its zone and its limits, scientific reasoning is an imperative which forms part of the authentic character of modern man. And when you hear, as you will have heard these last few years, and will be hearing for a few years more (though only a very few), someone say that he does not wish to reason or to think according to the demands of science, do not believe him; that is, do not believe that he really believes it, however much he shouts and even though he may seem disposed to let himself be killed for that pseudo belief. He is as little genuine as the one who now insists that science is everything, that science alone will save man, etc. That idea was genuine in 1883, but not today. The destiny, the life project, of European man today is mostly quite different from what it was a century ago. And this is because certain dimensions of our individual life are not those peculiar to any individual, but on the contrary those which are common to all; in the old phrase, they are "objective." There is no one form of thinking about numbers, of doing accounts, no separate form of mathematics for each individual man; but on the contrary, when man is thinking of numbers, when he is doing arithmetic, his own subjective truth, his genuineness, consists in the very fact of subscribing to the objective truth.

And this objectivity is not a matter only of science. With some small modification of meaning it also exists in other fields; in politics, for example. What modern man may decide on as his political opinion for the future is, whether we like it or not, not a matter of individual chance. There is a political authenticity which is common to all those living in each country, a general political "vocation." We may or may not be disposed to hear its call, but it sounds and resounds in our minds. And it would be curious, and symptomatic of the epoch, if that single authentic politique were represented everywhere today by a group which was important and clearly visible from afar. If this were true we would have a situation in which man was living a life which was subjectively false, was defrauding himself on the right as on the left. And as those of you who read are mostly young, I am sure that you will have plenty of time for events to clarify these slightly enigmatic words of mine.

But let us go back to where we were. As we carry within ourselves a "vocation" which is in great part common to all of us, which corresponds to the fact of our being contemporaries, we would only have to know how to listen to its voice and not alter it in order to be able to prophesy what the general lines of the future are going to be, at least the near future. How could this fail to be so, as we are the ones who are making the future, are creating it in our imaginations? The way in which each one foresees the future is, then, not so much a matter of looking beyond as of scrutinizing within one's most secret self. This task, this remaining alone with oneself and withdrawing into oneself, is of course one of the most difficult that can be attempted. The passions, the appetites, the interests ordinarily cry out with more force than does the "vocation," and they obscure its voice.

The other comment which I wish to make on this theme of the human power of prophecy, which is in essence the reverse of the human ability at history, is much shorter.

My intent was to study with some precision the European generations from 1550 to 1650. What I have to say about them is very different from what you are accustomed to hearing. Furthermore, my concept of history in general as a science, and of its concrete development as a historical reality, bears very little resemblance to the traditional treatment which you will find in any book. Consequently I had no other choice but to dedicate this volume to preparing you for the exposition of my exact theme. Therefore, I had to give you an idea of the reality which history investigates, that strange reality so close to us but so unknown which is called our life. Then I showed how the science of history ought to proceed in view of the genuine char-

acter of that reality, and why the method of investigation has to be the concept of the generation as the deepest root of historic change. From this there develops the
idea that man, in any historic reality, is always coming
from one world and going to another. The present is a
foreshortening of the past; and to analyze it is to see in
what is at hand the perspective of human destiny down
to the present date. As I have said, history cannot be
recounted excepting in its entirety. This was why it
was necessary for me to take you so great a distance
from my theme. In 1600 a new world was built on the
embers of the Middle Ages, athwart the Renaissance
crisis. In order to get to that we had to move ourselves
back to the origin of Christianity, to another period of
crisis. It was then useful to clarify the matter of what
historic crisis are in general, a highly dramatic matter
for us, as a large number of symptoms suggest that we
seem to be moving into one of these crises. Save for the
differences which each one shows, I have described certain phenomena which are fundamental and common to
the great crises which the West has suffered: that which
ends with the ancient world, that of the Renaissance, and
that which is now beginning.

With this background, I consider you well prepared
to understand the great human drama which begins in
1400 and ends in 1650, a drama of parturition which puts
on the planet a new man—modern man.

But as I was about to describe that drama to you, I had
to make you see why the medieval forms of human life
ended, and how the history of the fifth to the fifteenth
centuries is a ballistic trajectory in which man, impelled
toward the divine other-world by the force of desperation mounts upward in the Christian line to the thirteenth
century and then falls back onto the earth which he had
hoped to leave. But if we were justified in summing up

those ten centuries in a single chapter (given that the important thing for our purpose was to perceive what there was in them of trajectory, that is, of dialectic movement) we must slow our pace as we approach the period which I wish to clarify, the period of 1550. He who does not understand the fifteenth century well, understands nothing of what has happened since.

The fifteenth is the most complicated and enigmatic century in all European history up to our own day. And this not by chance nor for extrinsic reasons, but because it is the period of *the* historic crisis, the only true crisis thus far suffered by the new peoples of the west, those who surged out of another crisis, much older and graver, much more catastrophic, the crisis in which the culture of the ancient world succumbed.

The peculiar complexity of the fifteenth century comes from two causes. The first cause is that life within it, like life in all crises, is at its very root a dual existence. On the one hand is the persistence of medieval life, which still lives, or we may better say, survives. On the other hand is the obscure germination of new life. Two contradictory movements meet and collide in every one of those *quattrocento* men; medieval man falls like a skyrocket consumed and already ash. But out from this falling and inert ash there breaks forth a new rocket recently fired and mounting, pure heavenly vigor, pure fire, the energetic though confused beginning of a new type of living, of modern living. The shock between the dead and the living which is produced in midair results in the most varied combinations, all of them unstable and insufficient.

As I said before, man is always a coming from one thing and a going to something else. In periods of crisis this duality is converted into essential conflict; what he is coming from and what he is going to are completely antithetical, not like a normal exchange where yesterday and today are merely different stations on the same route, or different modes of the same basic attitude.

This man of the fifteenth century is, then, constitutionally the antithesis, the exact opposite of himself.

You already know what man means to me: not a soul and a body with its peculiar psychic and physical characteristics, but a specific drama, a precise life task. The psychological and corporeal characters in a man are secondary and do no more than modulate in various ways the argument of the drama. For example, man is first of all a Hamlet, and only afterward and secondarily the series of actors with different faces and different mannerisms who play this role. In this way history remains objective and not merely a series of jokes about the good or bad character of this man or that. It also ceases to be another thing, which we will discuss in relation to the best book (and within its limits a splendid book) thus far written about the fifteenth century, *The Waning of the Middle Ages*, by a Hollander named Johan Huizinga.

This fifteenth century man then is lost in himself, torn away from one system of convictions and not yet installed in another, without solid ground on which to stand; swinging loose on his hinges, so to speak, exactly as man is today. He still believes in the medieval world, that is to say, in the supernatural other-world of God; but he believes it without a living faith. His faith has already become a matter of habit, and inert, though this does not mean that it is insincere.

This matter needs a bit of analysis because it is essential to an understanding of modern and even contemporary man. Together with his customary faith in the supernatural, fifteenth-century man feels a new confidence in this world and in himself. Things begin to interest him, social tasks, other men; in short, nature for its own sake. Souls look simultaneously toward the one world and the other as though walleyed, belonging to neither; almost all the men representative of the fifteenth century are walleyed. And in their century we feel that peculiar disorientation which we feel in the company of a wall-eyed person: we do not know where he is looking.

His position with respect to all that he has come from is clear: pure Christianity has been exhausted, has given of itself as much as it could give. The oncoming wave of the Reformation will be no advance, no new formulation of medieval Christianity, but something which is already mundane and modern. But with respect to nature and the world, we do not see the position of this man clearly for the simple reason that he himself does not yet know what to do with his worldly environment; he has not yet gathered together a system of precise beliefs about it. The only thing he has clear is a desire for this world and a sense of illusion about it; already mobilized toward a worldly culture, he is like an arrow in flight toward its target. Thus, insofar as innovation is concerned, the attitudes of this century are understandable only if we keep constantly in mind the entire trajectory up to 1600, in which they appear mature and defined. To put it more concretely, in the entire fifteenth century there is perhaps no single thought worthy of a stable place in the human repertory of that which is clear and achieved. All thoughts of that period are guesses, conjectures, sluggish half-visions, hints, tendencies, attempts; in short, transitional. Humanity could fit itself within the system of ideas created by Galileo and Descartes because that ideology was composed of thoughts which had been fully worked out. In the ideology of the fifteenth century this was impossible, because it was composed of embryonic thoughts which were themselves mobile and moving toward a future perfecting.

The second reason why the study of this century is so complicated is an adjunct of the first.

Because this was a period not of installation in a world but of exodus from it, of peregrination toward a new world not yet achieved, the different peoples who form the great historical assemblage of Europe found themselves on different sections of the road, some well forward, others lagging behind.

You will note that insofar as historical matters are concerned, the earth has a different configuration in every period; that is, the different portions of the planet are articulated as in a topographic organism which is always different. Certain territories act like the vital organs of the general life of the times, while others are peripheral, like a muscle or a bit of fatty tissue. We can distinguish in the fifteenth century three peoples who act as organic centers, who send out solutions to the problems arising out of the general European environment; these are Italy, the Low Countries, and Spain, in that order.

Insofar as Europe's intellectual and sentimental evolutions are concerned, fifteenth-century Italy is the sector which is most advanced; in a way it is already outside the circle of medieval ideology. In the religious field, which is establishing continuity between medieval matters and the new way of living, the Low Countries represent the greatest advance. Fifteenth-century Spain is not far advanced religiously, intellectually, sentimentally, or esthetically. In those fields it finds itself behind France. But there is one dimension in which Spain achieves a greater maturity than all the other peoples of Europe: politics. The seeds of modern religion are scattered across the continent from the Low Countries, and the germs of the new science come from Italy; the modern invention of the state comes from Spain.

With all this complexity you will want to take note of my attempt to give you an idea of the form of life in the quattrocento. This is precisely the type of period in which the method of the generations becomes inevitable if one wants to compress events. Unless that method is vigorously applied, this century will never be understood. The same thing is true of the first century before Christ and the ones that follow. There was a reason why the historians of Christianity and the analysts of the New Testament had no other choice than to do as they did, and in fact, without paying much attention to what they were doing, without planning their investigations by generations, they managed to distinguish very well between the generations of the Apostles and those which followed.

Imagine that we were born around 1400. How would the business of living appear to us? We will believe in the Christian religion, that is to say, we believe that our lives depend definitely on an Infinite Being who demands of us a specific type of intellectual and moral behavior during our short journey through this world; or, what is the same thing, we must think certain things and do certain deeds or omit others. The list of what we must think about God and what we must or must not do is something that we cannot find out for ourselves or by our own means. It is not a matter of reasoning. God has revealed it to the Church. The dogmas and the commands are absurd, but they are a crude force of which we must take account. To cope with those irrational things, to accept them, however absurd they may seem to us, is faith for those of us who will study in the lecture rooms of the Occamists; the Occamists emphasize more than in any other period of Christianity the phrase *credo quia absurdam.* As far as the dogmas and the orders of the Church are concerned, we can do nothing but recognize them as one recognizes naked facts.

Our faith, then, is very different from that of St. Augustine, St. Anselmo, or St. Thomas. In questions of faith—and note this well—we are positivists. The Church says that one must believe this or do that out of faith (*de fide*); and there is nothing more to say. The supernatural is irrational because God is an absolute power who submits Himself to nothing save to not doing what in itself is contradictory. It would be too much to consider God rational, since reason is a purely human attribute. Thus, for example—and do not be surprised at me—God might very well take the form of a donkey, because a donkey is not a contradiction as is a squared circle. The leader of our professors, the genius Occam, sustained this textually although against many protests in his *Centiloquin theologicum: Non includit contradictionem Deum assumere naturam asininam.* And it would be great foolishness to think that Occam was not a most sincere Christian. Clearly, if that is possible, it will be no less possible that *quod ignis de potentia Dei absoluta potest recipere frigiditatem.*

This means that, except for what is directly contradictory, everything is possible if one thinks in the absolute; or, what is the same thing, there is no absolute reason why that which exists should exist and should be as it seems to be. What we call nature—the movement of the stars, the earth, ourselves—is pure contingency: it might not exist, or it might exist in another fashion. If we take things in the absolute, we will recognize that we do not stand on anything which is ultimately firm. Our only certainty is to have faith in God, to have faith without pretending to understand His being or His intentions. This is what faith is: complete trust and confidence. Not an evident belief that two and two make four, which is confidence in the certainty of things; our faith in God is a confidence *en bloc* which does not give us any confidence in respect to anything concrete. This is religious positivism. Let it be as God wills, because that is what God is—will, omnipotent will.

This renouncing of all absolutes in the field of reality gives our life an underlying stratum of resignation. Our faith is a little sad, even a bit melancholy. The fifteenth is the century of the melancholics. Though some men in Italy seem to become enthusiastic and even exalted over things of this world, we will find, if we look closely at that foreground flame, a background of melancholy of the soul into which they ultimately fall. This was the way that Lorenzo the Magnificent ended. And he was the man of the times, of the never-ending feasts, of the *triomphi*.

If the absolute is absolute arbitrariness and irrationality, what, then, is reality—earth, stars and their movements, the human mind? It is just what we have been saying— all that exists, and it is what it is because God has willed it so. The same is true of the dogmas. God could have revealed to us other dogmas the exact opposite of those which He did in fact reveal. The *credo* and natural reality are divine decrees, always susceptible of being abolished. Reality, then, is merely the contraction of the absolute power of God, *a potentia ordinata:* God could make any reality whatsoever, but in fact he fabricated this one. So we also find ourselves in a positivist attitude in confronting this world. St. Thomas and St. Bonaventura, believing that God is in good part intelligible because He is rational, could try to deduce the things of this world, its peculiar figure and its comportment, from Divine attributes. But there it is; we find ourselves holding an opposite form of belief and it seems to us that St. Thomas and St. Bonaventura suffered from an illusion.

We are certain that God made the world; but there everything ends, because at the same time we are certain that He did not do it for any reason. This matter of reason is a created human thing, an instrument which we possess in order to cope with nature, not with the supernatural. We begin, then, vaguely to suspect something tremendous which the previous centuries did not glimpse; that it is necessary to explain the things of the world from within the mundane, and to make a fundamental separation of faith from reason, of this world from the other. Man begins to live by double bookkeeping; he can no longer be only a Christian. God, precisely because He is God, does not serve us for walking through the world. The world, on the other hand, recovering this sudden independence, reveals a new attractiveness; that of having its own secret, separate and apart from the divine secret.

How little does our existence resemble that of the pure Christian, those primitive Christians who called themselves "the Saints"! Saintliness is no more than a form of life; it consists in living this entire life as if one were already in the next world. How? Very simple—we do not take anything that we do seriously, that is to say, we do not do it for its own sake; our concern with this, that, or the other will be a mere pretext for occupying ourselves with God. We reduce our existence to treating with Him. With the others we do not treat directly. We feel pain, and being only men, we have to be seriously occupied with that pain when it takes the form which we call suffering. Pain is then a negative thing. But if, in place of taking it seriously as something substantive and real in itself, we take it as something

which God sends us, then we transmute it, transfigure
it into something positive, so that the process of suffering it will be a joyful reality; and from the bitter heart
of the pain there will surge forth an unexpected thread
of delight.

The saint lives this life out of God and face to face
with God; that is, he starts toward things from the divine
point of view and he comes back with them to God.
It is a circular trip, a round trip to and from God. As
for things, the circular life of the saint is only tangential
to them: he touches them at one point, but he does not
let himself be overwhelmed by them, he is not impaled
on them. But we, if we continue living out of God, we
do it with faces turned to this world, and with no return trip. We come from God, but He stays at our
shoulder like the background of a landscape; meanwhile
we are mainly occupied with earthly things.

We can no longer fill our lives by occupying ourselves
with God because we have reached the belief that God
is unattainable by any direct route; He is the personifica-
tion of the over-there, He is what there is on the other
side of the horizon, that profile of the remote mountain
range which closes in our landscape, its role to be there
in the background, but a background to which we never
go. We go here or there within our own horizon, but not
over there; and if we did, it would cease to be over there.

I am trying, although perhaps vainly, to make clear to
you the complex religious attitude of the *quattrocento*
man, whose life structure we now wish to relive. The
consequence of his attitude is that in his state of religious
positivism man is uninterested in dogmas. And, in fact,
no one in the fifteenth century occupied himself with
dogmatic theology. Its source had dried up. It would not
flow again until a century after the Reformation and the
reaction against the Reformation which was symbolized

by the Council of Trent. Now, then; note well that that theology is occupation with the Divine Being, with its essence, attributes, and constituent mysteries. That is what preoccupied men from St. Augustine until the fourteenth century, at which time religion comes to consist of a very curious thing. A most fortunate phrase will reveal to us the secret of a new form of sainthood, an intraworldly form of sainthood, a religion which will not be theological, or dogmatic, or a living faith, but a matter of conduct in the world, as such. The phrase is this: *Imitation of Christ*.

The life which consists of imitating Christ is, first, disinterested in the question of whether God in His own Being, in His other-worldliness, is of this kind or that. Second, one single person is segregated from the Trinity —Christ. Third, one takes Christ, not in His character as a member of the Trinity, but as personifying the exemplary man. Thus, by a curious sleight of hand, we have reached a form of religion in which, if I am right, we have secularized Christianity by emphasizing in God His unique human intramundane facet. This does not mean that man goes outside of Christianity; on the contrary, man changes Christianity over to the human point of view and action. This is why I speak of secularization. And there rises in all Europe a strong religious disdain— note this, *religious*—directed against the ancient models of saintliness, of the perfect life; that is, against the friars and against the ecclesiastics in general. The new religion which inspired Thomas à Kempis began by being a religion of and for laymen, that is, the secular branch; the so-called "Brothers of the Common Life," of Deventer, in Holland, shed their influence over Germany and France and were the germ of the Reformation. Theirs is the *devotio moderna*. God is, for them, supremely the man, Christ; He is not even a priest. The most notable evidence in the case is that the original title of the *Imitation of Christ* was *De contemptu mundi*.

Nothing else will give you so keen an idea of the fact that life was about to change its center of gravity as this. No longer must life and the world affirm their right to existence in the face of religion; now the world as a particular kind of human life places itself inside religion and absorbs it. Ancient life was cosmocentric; medieval life was theocentric; modern life is anthropocentric. And next? You ask me without moving your lips, but in such a fashion that I hear it from here. With all the reservations and the modesty proper to such a grave matter, I will not hide from you the fact that I believe I know very well what kind of a life lies ahead.

But to continue.

The religion of the entire fifteenth century was made a matter of devotion, nothing more. The secular man, the man who lived in the world, was nauseated, bored, with friars and with ecclesiastics. He wished to treat with God in his own fashion; and as his fashion was mundane, his relationship with God consisted merely in a certain asceticism and a beauty of conduct in prayers and meditations which were very simple in content, but which maintained the soul in an almost permanent tenderness. This was a religion of sensibility; in fact, this is when man invented piety so great that it became bigotry. Such a thing was unknown in the Middle Ages. This secular man, although within the religious enclosure, rose up against the clergy, against the wise theologian. He despised wisdom: *The Imitation*, IV, 18, calls unnecessary the *altitudo intellectus neque profunditas mysteriorum Dei, beata simplicitas quae difficiles quaestionem relinquit vias et plana ac firma pergit semita mandatorum Dei*. Simplicity above all. Man was smothering in the theological and ecclesiastical underbrush. Again and again those devout laymen repeated the phrase *sacra ignorantia*. And since they decided to be ignorant, they did not need the clerics as intermediaries in their conversations with God. Furthermore, monasteries were founded in imitation of the secular houses of Deventer; and the prior who had most influence in the Middle Ages, Windeshein, adopted as a name John Know-Nothing. It is "the religion of souls" which they seek, not the religion of the intellect. They wished to weep. In fact, this is the century of tears. Everyone has mild and tender eyes, and everyone spends his life savoring the salty flavor of tears. In short, the dogma which is the belief in the most divine other-world-liness does not interest men; they seek the emotive state which is of this world.

One would have liked to hear what St. Augustine, who was a kind of wild beast of God, would have said to this *devotio moderna*. The softest phrase he would have used was, "That is more a morality than a faith." Century of the mystical, it was not creative, but kept swinging back to the ancient.

The fifteenth-century mystic, like the mystic of our own day, spoke little of God, but a great deal of those spiritual and corporeal states in which he was occupied with God. They reached the point of extreme manner-isms. Huizinga reminds us that "at table Suson, on eating an apple, used to cut it into four parts, eating three in the name of the most Holy Trinity and the fourth in a mov-ing recollection of the time when the Heavenly Mother gave the tender infant, Jesus, an apple to eat. And he ate his fourth part with the skin on because small children take great pleasure in eating apples without peeling them. In the days following Christmas itself, or perhaps during the time the infant Jesus was too young to eat apples, he did not eat the fourth part, but offered it up to Mary so that she could give it to her Son. What he drank, he took in five swallows to commemorate the five wounds of the Lord; but as Christ's side had gushed both blood and water, he would divide the five swallows in two."

To such a point did the worldly mannerisms of religion go.

Meanwhile the friars occupied themselves with hardly anything divine. The fall in their prestige was universal. A chronicler of the time, a personage who was at least pious, Molinet, in a poem celebrating the New Year, would say:

> *Prions Dieu que Jacobins*
> *Puissent manger les Augustins*
> *Et les Carmes soient pendus*
> *Des cordes des Frères Mineurs.*

All this is pure medieval Christianity come down to earth. Is it not also the religious situation of modern man? God—but in the background.

12

Renaissance and Return

On many counts it was necessary for me to emphasize the fact that in the fifteenth century the form of human living underwent a most radical change, although at the start the manifestations of that change were anything but radical; they were in fact very tenuous, and seemed solely a difference in tone. This radical change consisted of the fact that around the year 1400 man ceased to live within the folds of Christianity. The structure of man's life was no longer the rigorous one of existence within the Christian faith. For the first time in the evolution of European destiny, man's position became one of coming out of Christianity rather than of having his being within it.

And like everything else from which one comes, this remains at our backs. Man in the fifteenth century had been a Christian, as has our own age in a much more advertised form. Does this mean that he ceased to be one? To a certain extent. What we were yesterday or the day before, and have completely ceased to be—does this not form part of our present make-up? Certainly it does, certainly it continues to belong to us in the sense that it is a part of our being, but in the past tense. What we were yesterday has shaped our being and given it a certain style. When yesterday's content has volatilized, there still remains within us the mold and the style of that content.

Let me repeat again that the past goes on within the

present, and forms a part of it. European man was a Christian, as he was once a Platonist, as he was a Stoic, as he lived under the governance of Rome, as he was Paleolithic man; all that he was he continues to be, carrying it all as an abstract ingredient in his present character. The best proof of this lies in the fact that if man had lacked the basic experience of Christianity he would be very different today from what he is. Such is the inexorability of the precise destiny which man has suffered in the concrete course of history. It might have been another kind of destiny; but there it is, it was this kind, precisely this. And in that fact lies the interesting, the dramatic, the inescapable, element in the study of history.

In going down into the past we are merely descending into the caverns of our own existence. Therefore I find it important to show how one facet of our being which is still fully alive dates from the fifteenth century; this is the matter of having Christians behind us, of being Christians in the manner of men who were previously Christians, and who have come out of the faith. In the fifteenth century human life had a double root; and this, which brought about the unhappiness and the essential impurity of the Middle Ages, has by no means been eliminated in us: one lives a double game, a game of faith and a game of reason, even as one knows that these principles are antagonistic. And in the profound terms of historic reality, which I am now discussing, the present distinction between Christian and atheist is unimportant. Whether he likes it or not, the Christian of this modern and contemporary age must also be a rationalist and a naturalist, no matter what subterfuges and subtleties— I am talking only of those who are honest and loyal—he may use in order to reconcile the survival of faith within himself. And vice versa, the modern and contemporary atheist has in his life an important zone which neither reason nor naturalism can reach; he sees this zone, he feels it, he carries it within himself, however much he may struggle to deny it and to blind himself to its existence. That is to say, he believes without any concrete content of belief; he lives a faith now empty and uninhabited.

It is useful, then, to distinguish between being *in* something and being something. We are many things, but we are only present at, we only gravitate toward, certain of them. At any time the thing in which we are is by no means the thing that we most completely are. For example, it is indisputable that man today is in both economics and politics. Nevertheless, I wrote many years ago that after a period of obsessive preoccupation with economics and politics it would suddenly be discovered that both these disciplines are of the second rank; this is neither to say that they can be dispensed with, nor that to have had a certain success in them was, on the part of one who played those games without a clean conscience, not a crass error and subjectively false. We are still in that obsessive stage, and awaiting the fulfillment of the rest of the prophecy.

This inner duality and dissension between reason and faith is so habitual to us—to all of us, whether Catholics or irreligious—we are submerged in it in a fashion so inborn, that we do not perceive it very clearly. It is this that prevents us from placing ourselves in the position of the pure medieval man, the pure Christian whose life was at root unitary. I hope you will pardon me; but I do not permit a Catholic of our time to come to me and say, with a petulant air, that this transposition costs him no effort because he still continues to be the medieval man. Regarded with precision and clarity, such a statement is utterly false. Of course, as you know, I who am not a Catholic have about me no single trace of anticlericalism; indeed I think that to be an anticlerical is no point of pride, for today the only people who are anticlerical are those who cannot be anything else; it is a sign of personal lack of culture, and just as far removed from present-day reality as its opposite, to be proclerical.

But let me go on. The Catholic of the present moment, with all his fervent Catholicism, is today set in the modern world in a naturalist position. This situation is not an extrinsic passing through the world, but consists of being a part of that world, of carrying it within himself whether he wants to or not. The Catholic is vitally upheld by that naturalist position, is carried along by it just as is his opponent, with differences only of degree and of accident. He makes constant use of that position; he inhabits rationalism, he has his being within it; what happens is that he uses a part of himself to deny and combat it. Any man who is in a house, sheltered in it, lodged in it, may entertain himself by hitting at its walls in an effort to batter them down; but he does not thereby cease to be within the house.

In order to understand the position of Catholicism and of Christianity in general in our day, one should make the mental experiment of imagining in all seriousness that Catholicism by itself, and with no rival, were suddenly called upon to take the weight of all humanity. What is happening is, of course, the very opposite. Catholicism is in the opposition, which is always comfortable; and at any given time it takes what is convenient and accepts no responsibility for the rest. But in our imaginary experiment Catholicism would, for example, have to bear the weight of all the modern sciences, all of them—and note that I say the sciences and not merely the anticlerical speeches, which can be answered with miserable ease.

Let us not rail against destiny; it is useless. It is the destiny of modern man among other things that he must drag this internal duality along with him, giving heed to the double and contradictory imperatives of faith and reason.

Some time ago a socialist deputy made a speech in Oviedo, where for biographical reasons he was retracing the trajectory of his own experience. In it I find this phrase, and I cite it as I have cited texts of the thirteenth and fourteenth centuries: "this Socialist legion of ours, bound ever more closely by that new religious spirit, almost as strong now as Christianity, which is called labor solidarity." Why is it that this phrase—regardless of how accurate or inaccurate the fact it affirms—this phrase, with its echoes of St. Paul's Epistle to the Corinthians, rises through a trapdoor in the speech of a man who is so loudly and daringly an atheist? What is lacking, that he must create a new religion and compare it with Christianity? Why are political economy and socialism not enough for him? Why does he twist them out of shape in order to make something religious out of them?

It would be a mistake to think that this phrase is a matter of pure rhetoric, although there is certainly something of rhetoric in it. It is not pure rhetoric; and anyone who reads the first emotional paragraph of that speech not only discovers this, but finds an example which confirms my thesis. I refer to the paragraph in which he finds himself, as a child, in the proletarian quarters of Bilbao ". . . and there in that atmosphere my spirit was being formed, and turning over the very sad memories of an unhappy childhood, I made myself, I do not know whether quickly or slowly, as the strongest spiritual ties are built, I made myself the proposal, I promised myself, that all my life I would serve the underprivileged, the humble, the miserable among whom I found myself, and with whom I would always have strong spiritual bonds."

That, my readers, whether the socialist minister likes it or not, that is the essence of Christianity; it is Christianity *in vacuo*. If there had been no Christianity, it never would have occurred to this man to dedicate his life to anything. This is the fundamental thing in man's Christian life: to discover that life, in the last analysis, consists in having to be dedicated to something, not in busying oneself with this, that, or the other—which would be just the opposite, to put into life something which would be considered valuable—but in picking up one's entire life and surrendering it to something, dedicating it . . . this is Christianity's basic discovery, the thing which put it indelibly into history, which is to say, into man.

Ancient man was ignorant of this; for him the good life consisted at best of bearing the blows of fortune with dignity. At its finest this was Stoicism—life as a process of enduring, Seneca's *sustine*. But since Christianity came into being, man, however atheistic, knows and sees not only that human life ought to be the surrender of itself— that life takes on the sense of a premeditated mission and an interior destiny, the complete opposite of enduring an external destiny—but that whether we like it or not, life *is* this surrender. Tell me what else the phrase means which is so often repeated in the New Testament and is, like almost all the New Testament, so paradoxical: "He who loses his life shall gain it." That is to say, give your life, hand it over, surrender it; then it is truly yours, you have won it, you have saved it.

And this concept of life as the dedication of one's self to something, as a mission and not simply a discreet use of something which has been given to us, and given already made, has its opposite side; that life is then, in its own essence, responsibility for itself. Without Christianity, who would ever have made this discovery of life as responsibility?

Do not tell me that I have been talking of politics; I have been doing exactly the opposite. Out of a political speech—which like almost all of those of our day is a bit absurd and ridiculous—I have taken certain paragraphs and have managed to ennoble them by extracting from them their superpolitical secret heart.

I have chosen this example as I might have taken any other of our period; but it had to be done so that its own character of vulgar newspaper reality should serve as a vivid expression of that strange position in which man has found himself ever since the fifteenth century. Details of that position have, of course, changed enormously over five centuries; but even today one has only to close one's hand in order to catch and imprison a fact which perpetuates that manner of being a Christian even when one is no longer living it.

And throughout those five centuries we see a constant effort to fill the aching void in Christianity with something which is not Christianity: in the *quattrocento* itself men saw the start of what must be called *natural religion*. Cusanus hints at it. In his judgment the creeds of the different religions are, in the last analysis, equally true. God is unattainable—he wrote a book *De deo abscondito* —and our ideas about Him are the views of Him which we hold consistent in that we project our own peculiarities on Him. For underneath the different religions runs the unity of natural religion. Hence one can say: *Ego ingenium applicui ut etiam ex Alcoran evangelicum verum ostenderem.* Cusanus represents the start of the century. He was born in 1401. That vein of tolerance, almost eighteenth-century in spirit, will do no more than fatten in later generations even the Protestantism which slows it. Its extreme form—Bodin's *Colloquium Heptaplomeres*—will be a heinous work which could not be published. In this dialogue it is a Spaniard, Torralba, who represents the highest point of religious tolerance.

The deism of the seventeenth century is another attempt to fill the space in the European soul which Christianity left empty as it evaporated. The nineteenth century tried to theologize culture. We will see what our own is trying to do; whether it is trying, with a new creation, to overcome that basic duality of modern life which I find it so important to emphasize.

Because I was trying to show how fifteenth-century man ceased to dwell within Christianity as he had done during the Middle Ages, I dedicated the previous chapter to describing only the deepest and most sincere form of piety of which the period was capable. And we saw how even that *devotio moderna* was an effort to make faith worldly, a way of living from God outward, but with the face turned toward the world. By one route or another, and still without departing from the formal religious aspects of the fifteenth, sixteenth, and seventeenth centuries, we would see that man always goes toward the same goal, and in increasing proportion: he always ends by affirming this world. And this is the more curious when the intention seems exactly the opposite. Thus the thing that separated Luther from the Church was the worldly character of that same Church; for that reason he denied the ecclesiastical life as the true Christian life, and in its place affirmed the formally religious character of the life which was secular and without worldly preoccupations, in the form of work and profession. We serve God when we serve the world in the position and the vocation into which God has put us.

And the enemy of Protestantism, St. Ignatius Loyola, in order to combat it created an order which is the reverse of the traditional orders. The traditional orders proposed to carry man from this life to the next by the shortest road. Their discipline was the lever which pried man out of his worldly cave. They started from this life and headed for the next. The Jesuits, on the contrary, start from the other life in order to busy themselves with this one, in order to do battle with worldliness—and preferably where worldliness is at its most dense: in courts, in schools, in politics. Loyola's was the first modern order, and it brought with it all the symptoms of the new cismundane life. Hence its organization took as its model the most secular institution in existence, and the one farthest from mysticism—the army. The Company of Jesus is a Spanish *tercio a lo divino*. Opposed to Protestantism, it coincides with Protestantism in the vector of inspiration, thus revealing the identity of the period to which both of them belong.

If this was the religion of men who were dowered with a deep and personal religious vocation, those who by individual destiny would have been religious in any period, imagine how men who were not personally religious must have behaved during the fifteenth century, and particularly during its second half. On the ordinary man, the feeling of having for the first time got Christianity behind him had the effect of launching him on the world with appetites and a form of conduct so profoundly devoid of any religious flavor that one may unhesitatingly consider this the most irreligious period in the whole of European history. Unless this is noted, and another thing which I will tell you later, the Rome of the Borgias becomes unintelligible. The historian must not rest content merely with referring us to that tight warp of crimes; he must explain to us how it was that they were possible. Their most exaggerated stage came in the last years of the century, when the symptoms which would characterize the following century were already becoming clear. Let us, therefore, set this aside until we take up the sixteenth century.

I would like to leave in your minds a very brief but clear sketch of the first reactions with which Europe between 1400 and 1480 responds to the new situation, a situation consisting in the fact that men must now cope with their environment without the aid of a living faith, and therefore with means that are only human. For this purpose one may divide this century of transition into two parts: a first stage in which Gothicism still endures; and a second in which the so-called humanism comes to high tide.

Speaking strictly, here is what I call Gothicism: lay aside all that the world was to the later Middle Ages insofar as God was concerned—theology, mysticism, piety—and focus solely on what emerged from its thinking in regard to the more profane activities. That latter focus is what I call Gothicism. It consists, then, of the medieval world itself, but set as though independent of God. We have seen that this work of dissection, this leaving the world abandoned to itself, amputating it, or better, depriving it of communication with the afterworld of faith, was the task of the followers of Occam. At first this work had only the critical and negative intention to show that it is not possible to understand God's world by a process of deduction; and that this world, although created by God, is an absolute and naked fact with which one must come to grips and which lacks any principle or reason superior to that principle which would explain and establish it. Occamism, then, for reasons of technical detail which I now have no time to explain, did not immediately modify the face of the world; it merely cut its concrete relation with God at the root. The positive sense which it possessed, and which I set forth earlier, does not yet appear.

And in what kind of a world did that man who was a Christian in background find himself? Or, which is the same thing, what are his beliefs about this world? In the last analysis, it is the world which Aristotle thought out, but paralyzed and terribly complicated. Now one begins to see how little advantage was taken of Christian thought in the interpretation of things.

Let us try, as we did earlier, to relive that situation for ourselves.

Within it, we find ourselves living amid a belief which is almost completely opposed, as completely as can be imagined, to that which sustains man's life today. Today man sees nature as an infinite variety of phenomena which obey a certain very small number of principles. Physics nowadays is a science which is derived almost completely from one single principle. The entire physiochemical cosmos is a single homogeneous reality which, in the last instance, is reduced to mass, gravity, and time-space. For those of us who are now imagining ourselves to be man at the beginning of the fifteenth century, reality is far more complicated. Even setting aside the divine other-world, and looking solely at this one, we find it divided into two radically different ones: the world of the stars, the heavens; and the sublunar world of earth.

The difference between these two worlds, I repeat, could not be more complete and fundamental: the world of the stars is unchangeable and incorruptible; in the sublunar world, on the contrary, everything is born, dies, is subject to corruption. The reason is that this terraqueous world and all therein is made of matter; while in the sidereal world there is no matter, or if there is, it is an unchangeable matter, ether. The contraposition of characteristics as between the heavens and the earth does not end there. The movement of both worlds is contraposed. The stars move perennially with a circular and uniform movement which is the perfect movement, always equal to itself, without beginning or end. On earth, all natural movement is rectilinear, and consists in going from below up, like fire, or from above down, like a stone left to roll by itself. When earthly things do not move thus it is because their natural movement has been violently disturbed. This rectilinear motion of all sublunar things implies their peculiar finite character, for it must begin at one point and end at another, begin on the earth's surface, for example, and ascend to the fiery region underneath the sphere where the moon moves. Nothing can pass beyond that.

But this complexity of two such different worlds is multiplied by what is inside each one of them. The heavens are made up of fifty-five spheres. This many, or in a simpler interpretation, a few less, are needed to describe the movements of the stars in the heliocentric system.

If we now ask which, in all this about us, is the actual reality, whether in the heavens or on the earth, we meet this reply: reality lies in the substantive forms, which is to say, in the spiritual, the immaterial entities which inform matter—this combination produces those things which are perceptible. The Thomists believed that there was one of these forms for each kind of thing. The Scotists believed in a form for each individual in the species; that is, that there is a single form, "man," for all men, which is multiplied and individualized on contact with matter, or else that there will be in addition an individual form, "Peter," "John," or even "this Peter," "this John." The important thing is that these forms give birth to the phenomena; they are the reality of each phenomenon, and each one has nothing to do with the other; in this sense each is a reality, absolute and independent, and, in addition, immortal. Thus we find ourselves with a world built out of an enormous multitude of ultimate realities which are unvarying, indestructible, and independent. Let us take, for example, the simplest case, that upheld by the Thomists: this dog is born and dies because it is composed of the substantive form "dog" and of matter. But the form "dog" is in itself incorruptible, indestructible, and always identical with itself. One form cannot be changed into another; and as the world consists principally of forms, we will have to live in a world which tolerates no real transformation whatsoever. It is as it is, once and for all. There will always be dogs and horses and men, irremediably identical in every essential with what they are today.

And this way of thinking obliges us to interpret social life in a similar fashion. Society is composed of ranks which cannot be destroyed. There are kings, nobles, soldiers, priests, there are countrymen, businessmen, artisans. All this is and forever will be, world without end, indestructibly, each social figure enclosed within itself. And thus with the prostitute and the criminal.

In regard both to material nature and social matters, modern man holds opposite beliefs. He thinks that the very essence of reality is transformation, and that there is no such thing as *the* dog, *the* horse, *the* man. Reality consists of things which are going to be approximately dogs, in order later to be turned into horses or men, or other things not now existent. Just as he does not believe that the stars are immutable, but are in a state of evolution, are formed, expand, and succumb in order that they may give way to unsuspected heavens, so he also believes that the living being is pure and constant change, from the simple infusoria all the way up to man. Up to man? No, much farther; for this modern concept, which makes reality consist of pure transformation, recognizes that what has been up to now is by no means all that there ever will be. Reality is not closed and reduced to the past and the present, but holds open the frontier of the future, in which the real will be something that has not yet come into being.

The medieval universe was made up of absolutes. Each thing was what it was, and nothing more, for it was indestructible. Today nothing is what it is, but stands always in a state of transition toward being in another wise. Each thing can be something else, everything has in it a little of everything. We are in the era of the cats that are neither black nor white, but gray. At the start of the fifteenth century even the social ranks themselves, the offices and the professions, were absolute. There was the bishop and the archdeacon, the canon, the pastor, the student, the prince, the nobleman, the gentleman, the merchant, the married man, the widow, the damsel, the religious. In the book written by Dionysius the Carthusian, *De doctrina et regulis vitae christianorum*, one can see the absolute and as it were, the eternal definition of all these forms of human reality which must always be taken into account. And note that the author is one of those nearest to the greatest genius of this period, the man who really anticipated the entire Renaissance, the great Cusanus, who went trotting tirelessly through the world with two intimates at his side; on the one hand this inexplicable graphomaniac, Dionysius the Carthusian, and on the other the attractive figure of the Spaniard Juan de Segovia, whom I know to be completely unrecognized in Spain and who is cited here for the first time.

This seems to me a splendid example of what I have called variations in the structure of human life, in the drama that is living. Because it is obviously a very different task to live in an unchanging world where everything is absolute from what it is to live in an environment where, in principle, nothing is absolute and everything can change. And it shows lack of comprehension to claim that everything is reduced to the fact that man changes his ideas about things. No, on the contrary. If, as has been commonly believed, ideas were the only things that

changed, the change would not be serious. But the difficulties lie with the problem of life, which each of us
must go on resolving as long as he lives, and which is completely different when one lives amid one set of ideas
from what it is when one lives amid another.

If we lived in the nineteenth century, believing that
nothing around us has final and absolute reality and that
everything, material as well as social, is susceptible of
change we would react to every difficulty by managing
to transform that troublesome reality to our own liking.
In this sense modern man is at bottom revolutionary—
we will see how revolutionary when we come to Descartes. And vice versa; while man may be revolutionary,
he is still only modern man, he has not risen above modernity.

But if we lived in the fifteenth century and were facing
a period of anguish, a worry or a conflict, the last thing
that would occur to us would be to transform into something else a reality which would seem to us essentially
untransformable. What, then, could we do? You see how
this imaginary emigration into another age, this mental
experiment which we make when we think of having to
exist in the year 1440, brings us violently up against the
basic difference between historic reality then and now.

And note also that in the early years of the fifteenth
century we must live in a world which is too well known,
too old, with all its corners too much trodden, a world
of crowding complexities which oppresses and smothers
us. Nothing about it has the inciting grace of novelty;
everything is what it was and what it will go on being,
without remedy, without hope. The Church, the State,
the University with its science, social life, domestic habits,
games—everything is ritualized, everything is formulae,
and almost sacramental. In this sense our problem is not
to know what we must do in every case; the misfortune

here is the reverse: for every step we take, we know in advance precisely what must be done. For every single eventuality a canon is already established, in the most minute detail; and those details are infinite in number. The only difficulty, and the one most productive of despair, is the having to learn, to absorb, this most complicated ritual. When we go to the University we know ahead of time that we will be taught nothing new, that we will have to ingurgitate mountains of definitions, of distinctions, of subtleties, which are purely formal. The Occamites who protested in metaphysics that the principles or *entes* were multiplied unnecessarily were at the same time carrying to a supercharged and grotesque extreme the multiplication of distinctions in logic, which was the field that interested them.

Everything had become an inert and most complicated topic—law, administration, science, theology. Culture, instead of being a clear and quiet repertory of solutions for life, had become clouded, had been turned into a memorandum book, a manual. The Spanish word for it comes out of this period. *Mamotreto* comes from *Mammetrectus*, the name of a voluminous commentary on grammar which weighed heavy on the youth of the best men of the fifteenth century. Erasmus had an irrevocable hatred of it; and in his dialogues and letters he piled up jokes and sarcastic remarks about it, assuring it a bad reputation which has given it a kind of immortality.

As you can see, the man who lived in such an atmosphere found himself between the sword and the wall. At his back and behind him lay a lifeless Christianity, paralyzed, formulist, lacking in any living faith. Before him lay a world which could not possibly be transformed into any other kind of a world. This is the dimension, the characteristic, which most profoundly differentiates that period from our own time, a distinction which must be emphasized now that we have discovered so many other surprisingly similar characteristics. In the fifteenth century, as during the whole of the Middle Ages, man lived with a horizon which was closed toward the future, not only because he conceived the world as a reality that did not vary, but even more concretely because he believed that it was nearing its end. Hence the frequency with which Europe became perturbed, fearing that at this date or that the world would come to an end. The old idea that human destiny had run through the four universal monarchies still ruled; and with this belief was mixed the interpretation of the Latin Floro. He applied to past history the four ages of man, and hence announced that the Roman Empire, of which medieval Europe considered itself a mere continuation, represented old age. This is what I mean by saying that they lived between the sword and the wall. Only in Bacon's generation, and more basically in that of Descartes—between 1580 and 1620— did human life redress the balance and find that the past weighed less than the future. This is the turning point. Modern man orients himself in the future, and not—like the man of the Middle Ages and indeed the ancient world —in the past. Jorge Manrique expressed the ancient and medieval attitude by saying that any period that was past was better. Bacon and Descartes were the first ones who really believed the opposite: that the future would be better, if for no other reason than because it would be the future.

But in imagining the fifteenth century we must keep our eyes turned from the future, which was then hermetically sealed, and focus our attention on the then present. In this situation only two types of attitude will fit:

One, the most commonplace, will consist in accommodating ourselves to the traditional world, known and

worn though it is, and in finding out how to get pleasure
out of it, exaggerating it, carrying its complications to
an extreme, creating on top of it a series of ceremonial,
ornamental, and symbolic conventions. In short, over-
loading it, heaping it with mannerisms. This was Gothicism, florid Gothic, or as the French say, flamboyant.
Given that the substance of life cannot change and that
its constant repetition has dulled us to it, let us live by
adding adjectives to it, emphasizing that reality which
has forever existed. In short, let us live as if these substances were mere symbolic formalisms, duplications, as
it were, of real life on a plane of conventions, as is done
in a play. Certain roles are agreed upon and accepted as
though they were realities.

For example, let us emphasize the reality of the professions with costumes peculiar to each guild. Gothicism
was the period of uniforms; it delighted in long proces-
sions and corteges in which each state, class, and office
paraded with representative pomp. Because we must all
irremediably live one with another, given that nothing
that is can truly be destroyed, we take pleasure in con-
templating ourselves spectacularly, giving external and
plastic emphasis to the invisible substantive form which is
the deep reality within every reality. The most modest
people take advantage of any pretext to show themselves
their essential pluralism. When Don Juan II goes to marry
his son to Doña Blanca of Navarre, this Princess with her
mother the Queen passes through Briviesca: "There" says
the chronicle, "festivals had been made ready, and there
was a very solemn reception by everyone in the city,
each trade displaying its banner and its symbolic performance as best it could; and after these came the Jews
with the Torah and the Moors with the Alkoran," etc.
It is clear that we are in a humble Castilian town (Cas-

tilian villages are apparently condemned to be eternally humble) and not in the great rich cities of the period, in Antwerp or Ghent or Dinan.

But note this: the Jew was there, too, with his sacred book, and the Moor with his Koran. This means that every human being had the right and the duty to be what he was—the great and the humble, the pious and the damned. For medieval man, the Jew and the Moor were realities with full rights in the rank and positions set for them within the hierarchic pluralism of the universe. In the early years of the fifteenth century it would not occur to anyone to suppress the Jew or the Moor. This did occur to the generation of the Catholic monarchs— the generation of 1450.

What a change! Who belonged to this generation? Fernando was born in 1452, which is just when Leonardo was born; Erasmus and Machiavelli around 1462. They are enough. This is the first modern generation. And, in point of fact, the expulsion of the Jews and the Moriscos is a typically modern idea. The modern believes that he can suppress realities and build the world to his liking in the name of an idea. In this case, it is the idea of the state which the Catholic kings were initiating. Hence those who today expel the Jews in the name of a return to the Middle Ages are committing a lamentable *quid pro quo*. We moderns can hardly comprehend the substantial tolerance of medieval man.

This way of living not only real life, but also its duplicate in a phantasmagoria of figures, symbols, and rituals which express it, was the only way which the common man had of enriching his existence, caught as he was between the sword and the wall. He augmented and modified it vertically, so to speak. If this seems absurd to us, it is because we have the future still open, and we can enrich, improve, and change our life the full width of its dimension, that is to say, horizontally.

But the best men of that day did not accept that solution. The life about them, insincere, overloaded, lived according to formula, did not, in their minds, merit being affirmed and accepted. On the other hand, there was no room for a true transformation, a new life. The real forms were perennial. But it was possible to reduce them to their original purity, to clear them of excrescences, of additions, of adjectives. In short, though life cannot be transformed, let us return to its pure forms. This is the reform, as distinct from the revolutionary, spirit—it is the return of the primitive form. And this is what all the words that imply struggle and effort which were heard on the best lips—*reformatio, restitutio, renasci, renovatio*—really signify. *R*enovation is not *in*novation; on the contrary it is a return to being, precisely and with no change, what something was in the beginning.

Such is the spirit in which religious reform and humanism began. These were not impulses toward the future, but quite the opposite. With the future closed, and some change compulsory, the only thing possible is return. One returns to the ancient world, not only to Greco-Roman culture as such, but to the entire primitive world. Petrarch, sounding the tocsin for a return to antiquity, includes not only the classics, but also the fathers of the Church. Conrado Altis mixes the resurrection of the Greeks and Romans with that of primitive Germanism; and Erasmus dedicates himself to editing the Fathers of the Church and the first books of Christianity.

But I shall have to stop on the threshold of this new form of life, reformist and humanist, which is going to triumph in the second half of the fifteenth century. There was not time enough.